I0815798

THE Zen Guide TO Opening Your Heart

THE Zen Guide to Opening Your Heart

Practical Advice from a Buddhist Monk

GENSHO TAIGU

Chief Priest of Fukugonji Temple
and Bestselling Author

TUTTLE Publishing

Tokyo | Rutland, Vermont | Singapore

Contents

CHAPTER 2
How to Break Through the Wall of Anger

CHAPTER 3
How to Break Through the Wall of Ignorance

CHAPTER 4
How To Overcome the Wall of Wanting

CHAPTER 5

How to Change Your Mental Habits

23 Positive Mental Factors and 13 Neutral Mental Factors in Buddhism

Lessons for a Lighter Heart

It's nice to make your acquaintance. My name is Gensho Taigu, and I serve as the chief priest of Daisozan Fukugonji Temple in Komaki City, Aichi Prefecture, Japan. Every day, through YouTube and other media, I offer guidance and support to those who are struggling. I often receive messages like these:

> *"Bad things seem to happen every day and I don't know how to cope."*
>
> *"I can't stop thinking about my past mistakes, and it's breaking my heart."*
>
> *"Life is too hard. I wish I were dead."*

At the moment, there are more than two thousand people waiting to speak with me. This number is an indication of the challenges that people face in the modern world—the burdens they carry and the pain they endure. Through years of listening to people's worries and suffering, I've come to realize something fundamental: all suffering originates from the same source. Yet, most people remain unaware of this truth.

To put it plainly, all the suffering that arises in the heart is born from illusions we create in our own minds. Our suffering is not created by other people.

Some may find this idea hard to accept:

"That's not true! My boss makes my life miserable!"

"My husband is cheating on me—why is that my fault?"

But consider this: the boss you detest or the unfaithful spouse is only the catalyst. The suffering itself arises from your own mind—your thoughts, your emotions and your interpretations of the situation. You might be thinking that if that's the case, there's nothing you can do about it. But rest assured—there is a way forward. This is precisely where Buddhism can be of great help. Unlike religions that promise salvation through faith alone, Buddhism is centered on awakening to the truth. The word Buddha means "one who has awakened," referring to Shakyamuni after he attained enlightenment. Shakyamuni—also known as Gautama Siddhartha—lived over 2,500 years ago in India. After his profound spiritual awakening, he became known as the Buddha.

The central focus of Buddhism is the mind. By facing your own mind, closely observing its movements and reactions, and calmly analyzing the ebb and flow of your emotions, Buddhism guides you toward releasing suffering and cultivating a stable, peaceful heart.

Despite being over 2,500 years old, the teachings of the Buddha remain profoundly relevant today. If we embrace this way of thinking, we can ease our burdens, find solutions to even the most difficult problems, and gradually transform our outlook on life.

I speak from experience. There are times when I, too, have felt lost—when I made serious mistakes, faced failures in business and even questioned whether I wanted to go on living. But time and again, the teachings of the Buddha have guided me through.

It takes courage to look inside ourselves and challenge the assumptions, fears and comparisons that trap us in suffering. But by breaking down these inner walls, we can free ourselves from unnecessary pain.

Of course, negative emotions—anger, sadness, jealousy, anxiety—can never be entirely erased. We are human, after all. Some emotions, like anger, can be harmful, while others may serve a purpose. The key is learning to recognize the difference and manage them wisely. By understanding the emotions that cause suffering, acknowledging them and letting them go, we can move through life with greater ease and peace of mind.

This is not an overnight transformation. Developing the mindset to overcome inner struggles takes time. But even small shifts in perspective can lead to profound change. Over the years, I have seen countless individuals reshape their lives simply by learning to see their problems differently.

In this book, I will share practical methods to help you break through your own "inner walls." While my teachings are rooted in Buddhist philosophy, I have made them accessible so that anyone, regardless of background, can benefit from them.

Life contains more suffering than pleasure—that is undeniable. But even in the midst of pain, we can learn to reduce its grip on us and increase moments of happiness, joy and contentment. If this book can become one of the lights that illuminate your life, nothing would make me happier.

Where Suffering Begins

What kind of impression do you have of Buddhism? Many Japanese people may define it as a religion where believers chant the nembutsu and pray to the Buddha. But the essence of Buddhism is not about worshiping a deity or seeking external salvation. As mentioned in the foreword, the heart of Buddhism is about looking within. It is a philosophy of self-exploration that helps us reduce worry and suffering, guiding us toward a life of inner peace and positivity.

Unlike other religions that emphasize devotion to a higher power, Buddhism is rooted in self-awareness. The Buddha realized that human suffering arises from our desires—our endless pursuit of more. The greater the desire, the greater the suffering.

> *"I want to get into a good school and get a good job at a good company."*
>
> *"I want to marry someone successful."*
>
> *"I want to make lots of money, live in a big house and live an easy life."*

In modern terms, these are the kinds of desires we are talking about.

"I want this, I want that" – this is the root of your suffering.

People think that if these desires are fulfilled, they will be happy. However, these cravings are endless. Even if you get one thing, you will want something else, and you will inevitably compare yourself to others and want more and more. And this craving for "more" is what increases your suffering.

As long as you look outside yourself for the cause of your suffering, your suffering will never disappear, and you will never be happy either. The Buddha discovered this. He taught that if you really want to be happy, you need to look inside yourself, at your heart, and change your way of thinking.

In other words, if you can overcome the "walls in your heart," you can let go of your worries and live with a more peaceful soul.

The Key to Happiness is within Yourself

The effort required to try to overcome the walls in your heart is perhaps a little different from the kind of work we usually associate with the word "effort." I think many of us have been brought up to think we should put effort into working hard to earn more money than other people, obtain the material things we desire and live a financially comfortable life.

I'm not saying that this is wrong, but the kind of lifestyle where you seek happiness from something outside yourself and become dependent on it can lead to suffering. In contrast, Buddhism teaches us to focus inward—to make the effort to let go of the suffering in our hearts. And the Buddha showed us the method to do just that. This is what he said:

> Life is entirely filled with suffering. In other words, everything begins with suffering, so we

> must accept that fact. To do so, we must develop wisdom, let go of the suffering we carry and live brightly and cheerfully. Life is a series of hardships. Since we can't escape the pain of aging, sickness and death, let's face reality thoroughly and live as joyfully as we can.

In simple terms, that is the message the Buddha left us.

Buddhism is not about "becoming happy by simply following the teachings of God" or "being saved by believing in something." Instead, it offers a way of thinking and living—a practical method—based on the idea that if you think and act in certain ways, you can let go of worry and suffering.

As we will discuss in Chapter 5, the Buddhist prescription for curing suffering is to abandon negative thoughts and emotions ("negative mental factors") and cultivate positive thoughts and emotions ("positive mental factors").

In this method of healing, we are not trying to cure the symptoms of the problem, we are looking at the cause. Even if it is difficult to put everything in this book into practice, if you can just try following a few of the steps, you will start to open up a world that is easier to live in than the one you are living in now.

There are many people who think Buddhism is similar to Adlerian psychology, especially those who have only recently started studying Buddhism. But his should actually be the other way around. It is not that Buddhism is similar to Adlerian psychology, but that Adlerian psychology is similar to Buddhism.

The psychologist Alfred Adler was born in 1870, and it was not until the beginning of the twentieth century that he began to advocate his particular brand of psychology. In contrast, the

Buddha established Buddhism around 2,500 years ago, in the fifth century BC.

It is true that both Adlerian psychology and Buddhism share the same basic theme of letting go of suffering so that we can achieve inner peace. In the early twentieth century, when Adler was active, the study of Buddhism was popular in Europe and exerted an influence over many scholars, and it is likely that Adler too could have been influenced by Buddhism to some extent.

The Basic Stance of Buddhism

In Buddhism, there is a system of learning called "Three Baskets" (Tripitaka). This refers to the essential attitude for studying Buddhism and the disciplines that must be learned. The system is made up of three parts: Sutra, Vinaya and Abhidharma.

The Sutra refers to the Buddha's teachings. The Buddha, who attained enlightenment at the age of thirty-five, spent forty-five years walking around preaching and saving people from suffering until his death at the age of eighty. The disciple who accompanied the Buddha and heard his teachings more than anyone else was Ananda. The Sutra are the teachings of the Buddha that were compiled by Ananda after his death.

The Vinaya refers to the rules and code of conduct for the community. The Buddha advised his disciples with teachings like: "If you're alone, you'll slack off. If there are two of you, you'll end up fighting. If there are three of you, you'll split into two opposing groups. So, gather together in groups of four or more, and help and encourage each other as you train." The

Wisdom from 2,500 years
ago can be a tool
to let go of
today's worries.

Buddha encouraged his disciples in this way. This group of practitioners is called the Sangha. When four or more people gather together, it is only natural that they will have different backgrounds and ways of thinking, so it is necessary to have rules to ensure that everyone can live together in harmony and without conflict—and that is what the Vinaya provides.

The Abhidharma consists of commentaries on the Sutra and Vinaya, or the independent theories about them developed by later disciples.

As mentioned earlier, these three elements of learning—Sutra, Vinaya and Abhidharma—are collectively referred to as "Three Baskets," and a Buddhist monk who has mastered all three is called a Tripitaka Master. The character who appears in the Chinese novel *Journey to the West* (widely known in English-speaking countries as *Monkey*, translated by Arthur Waley) is called Tripitaka but the name is a general term that has been used many times in history for this type of monk.

Buddhism Teaches How to Let Go of Suffering

Now, here's the main topic. In the final Abhidharma treatise of the Three Baskets, there is a commentary that provides a detailed analysis of the human mind. To put it simply, it's a textbook on Buddhist psychology. In this, my own book, I attempt to convey a gentle explanation of the "way to let go of suffering" that appears in the Abhidharma, avoiding the use of difficult Buddhist terminology as much as possible.

You may be wondering if teachings from 2,500 years ago can still be applied today. Don't worry. It is precisely because these teachings are so effective that Buddhism has been passed down through the years without interruption. And many psychologists throughout history have also used Buddhist teachings as a reference.

Buddhism explains in a systematic and extremely logical manner how the problems and sufferings we experience come about, what their nature is, and how these sufferings can adversely affect our bodies and minds. And most importantly, the question, "How do we let go of suffering?" is answered with remarkable clarity and detail, laid out in a thoroughly reasoned and structured way.

What's more, these ancient insights align closely with what modern scientists have discovered through years of research, and with what psychologists now commonly accept as standard practice. The Buddha had already reached this understanding 2,500 years ago.

The Buddha is the Master of the Heart

Professional soccer players are masters of their sport. Iron chefs are masters of cooking. The Buddha is the master of the heart. It is the role of monks such as me to learn the Buddha's teachings, put these teachings into practice, and then pass them on to people who are troubled. Rather than studying Buddhism as an academic subject, we build it up as a form of training to discipline the mind. This is what we call "practice."

I didn't study psychology anywhere, but I think that I am able to advise those who come to me with their troubles because I have studied and practiced the teachings of the Buddha. The practical and effective guidelines from Buddhism that form the basis of this book will surely help to resolve your worries and anxieties.

There is a Buddhist verse that simply and clearly summarizes the teachings of the Buddha:

Do no evil.
Do good deeds.
Purify your heart and keep it pure.
This the teaching of the enlightened Buddhas.

So then, what is evil? What is good? What exactly do these words mean? When I talk about this poem, I often get asked questions like these.

The terms "good" and "evil" here refer to moral good and evil. The word "good" can also be translated as "skillful," and the word "evil" as "bad" or "unskillful." So another way of rendering this verse might be:

Live by a moral code.
Stop doing bad things and live skilfully.
And keep your heart pure.
This is what the Buddha taught.

In our daily lives, we carry out most of our actions unconsciously. For example, when we walk, we alternate between our right and left feet, and we shift our center of gravity and balance from side to side, but we don't have to think about these actions one by one. We can move our bodies intuitively. However, progressing from crawling to walking when we are babies is quite difficult. But by gradually accumulating the knack of how to move, a baby becomes able to stand up and walk. In the same way, even actions that we can now do unconsciously are the result of small efforts and repetitions over time.

What is the difference between those who live skillfully and those who do not?

So, what if there were things we were doing unconsciously that were "unskillful"? What if we were unknowingly accumulating "bad ways of doing things"? If these are done unconsciously, they are not so easy to fix.

So, what should we do?

The key is to bring those unconscious patterns into your conscious awareness. What is important is that you yourself become aware of what is unskillful.

Change Your Beliefs, Change Your Destiny

You've probably encountered situations in your everyday relationships that make you feel like this:

> *"For some reason, the way that person talks really gets on my nerves."*
>
> *"I know what they mean but their tone makes me uncomfortable."*

I think that these situations are quite common. Even if someone is saying something completely reasonable, if their way of speaking is unskillful, they can leave a negative impression. Many people are not conscious of their tone of voice, behavior and mannerisms.

The way you speak is something that is being sent outward, so one way of fixing it is when other people notice it and point it out, giving you a chance to improve. Since only you yourself can understand your own thought patterns, in order to become "skilled" you have to be aware of your own weak points. As Mahatma Gandhi famously said:

Your beliefs become your thoughts,
Your thoughts become your words,
Your words become your actions,
Your actions become your habits,
Your habits become your values,
Your values become your destiny.

We tend to look only at the "destiny" part and lament our misfortunes. But doing so doesn't change anything. Unless we change our fundamental beliefs, we cannot change the destiny that follows.

The beliefs we hold are unconsciously formed through the influence of various things around us, such as our family, friends, acquaintances and the media. Everyone thinks, speaks and acts based on these unconscious beliefs, and these beliefs determine our character and destiny.

The Buddha sought to transform those very beliefs and mental frameworks that lie at the root of who we are.

Of course, it's not easy to change a belief that you've built up since childhood. But if you really want to change your destiny and your life, you have no choice but to go back to the starting point. And, if you can change the root, you can let go of all your current worries and suffering.

For example, maybe you have trouble communicating with the people around you and are not good at socializing. If you just keep thinking "It's not my fault, I was born with this personality," or "I can't get on with anyone," you won't be able to change anything. It might be more helpful to try and develop the belief that "I should be grateful to the people around me and try to show them my gratitude, even if I can only express that little by little."

Even if it's something small, try to have the thought, "I'm

grateful for this," and then express it out loud by saying "Thank you." By doing so, the way the people around you see you, and their attitude toward you might change, and you may find that they start talking to you and that channels of communication start to open up.

This is an example of how you can change your personality and your destiny by changing your thoughts, words, actions and habits, based on the belief that you should be grateful to others.

Buddhism is a packaged "method of awareness" to help you to look at yourself clearly.

The Buddha was born into a royal family and grew up in a privileged environment where he never lacked for food, clothing or shelter. Nevertheless, he was plagued by worries and suffering, and he abandoned everything to bring about reform in society and become the founder of Buddhism.

As long as we are human, we cannot escape certain truths. Everyone has worries and suffering, even when they seem to live in enviable situations, like these people who contact me through my YouTube channel, *Osho Taigu's One Question & One Answer*:

> *"I have an inheritance that I can't use up even if I tried for the rest of my life."*

> *"I live in a big house, my husband is the director of a listed company and my children attend a prestigious school."*

You might think, "Where is there any worry or suffering in

Even those who seem blessed
have their own worries
and suffering.

a life like that?" but people like these are not immune from pain. Even people who appear to have everything may still question the meaning of their life. For example, compared to the war-torn Japan of eighty years ago, Japanese people today don't have to worry about what they eat or what they wear. After the war, the so-called three sacred treasures—refrigerators, washing machines and televisions—became widespread, and labor-saving electrical appliances continued to evolve. These days, everyone has a smartphone, even elementary school students.

If we look at our society from the perspective of the time when the Buddha was alive, the standard of living we enjoy today is equivalent to that of a king. But if you ask someone if they're happy or if they have any worries, they are more than likely to complain about something.

Despite the fact that daily life has become more convenient and the world has become a better place to live, people are not necessarily any happier. There are unavoidable worries and suffering for everyone—anytime, anywhere.

Even with Wealth or Fame, There Is Still Suffering

Even if we were to obtain the kind of lifestyle and environment that we believe would make us happy, we would still inevitably experience problems and suffering. Even if we gain wealth and amass possessions, our desire for more and more will probably never be satisfied.

When we see news reports on television about the suicide of a celebrity who seemed to have achieved success and was living a glamorous life, it is not uncommon to find ourselves involuntarily exclaiming, "No way. That person?"

I was once asked by a record company to introduce a new

song by American singer songwriter Billie Eilish on YouTube as part of a promotional campaign. It's said that she struggled with severe depression and even harbored suicidal thoughts, to the point that her mental state had significantly deteriorated. At the age of nineteen, she had become the youngest person ever to win the Grammy Award for Record of the Year for two consecutive years. Even a top star with a spectacular career, an artist at the height of her popularity, can suffer from depression.

In addition to celebrities, there are also many cases of people in professions that everyone admires or envies, such as professional athletes and doctors, who are living with inner struggles we can't see. Even people who are blessed with enviable circumstances have their own worries and suffering. To come to terms with these worries and suffering, we need to understand the workings of the heart so that we can better protect it.

In the Buddhist scriptures written in the ancient Indian language of Pali, the word *dukkha* appears frequently. This word can be translated as "suffering."

When we hear the word "suffering," we probably imagine negative emotions such as anger, hatred and sadness. But even things that appear to be positive or good, such as joy and pleasure, are actually dukkha. In other words, joy and pleasure are also suffering. This is what the Buddha taught. Although this may sound confusing, dukkha is not a negative expression. Dukkha expresses a state of "constant change and no stopping."

We tend to think that the opposite of joy is suffering, but both joy and suffering are merely transient stimuli that appear and disappear in the heart. This is easy to understand if you think about it in terms of the pendulum principle. If your

All worries are transitory.

emotions swing in a negative direction, you will suffer, and if they swing in a positive direction, you will be happy. But the emotion of joy is not eternal. For example, let's say you have a crush on someone and when you confess your feelings, they say they feel the same way. This is a very happy event, so your joy explodes. You really hope that this love will last for a hundred years.

But romance is not all fun and games, and in most cases, a relationship will eventually come to an end The more you love someone, the more happy memories you have of them, and the greater the sadness you feel when you lose them, and this can move you toward suffering with great momentum, like a pendulum.

Ultimately, your heart is most stable when it is in a balanced state, neither swinging to joy nor to sadness.

In Buddhism, "peace of mind" means to always look at your own heart, to know that it has a range of ups and downs, and then to be able to bring it to a stable state.

Neither Joy Nor Suffering Last Forever

People who have a romantic view of love, and believe that the ideal situation is to always be in that lovey-dovey state that characterizes the start of a relationship, often find themselves suffering more the longer they stay in a relationship.

People who work hard and feel the need for constant self-affirmation and strive to be positive at all times will probably suffer from not being able to always be in that state.

There is no absolute value for joy or sorrow. You may try

to live your life by absolutely believing in what is supposed to be "better" or "the way things should be." You may strive to always be in love with your partner, or to become a person with high self-esteem, or to spend each day with a positive attitude. But if you do this, the chances are that you will actually end up moving further away from happiness.

Of course, when you are happy, you should enjoy it. But you also have to understand that the happiness won't last forever. And the same is true for suffering. Suffering does not go on forever either. In Buddhism, it is believed that everything that exists in this world is temporary. All phenomena are constantly changing, never maintaining the same form. This truth is referred to in Buddhism as "the impermanence of all things."

Nothing lasts forever.

Where there is pleasure, there is pain. But where there is pain there is also pleasure. And, of course, both pleasure and pain are things that arise within ourselves. They are things that are within our own control.

Let's start by learning about how this works.

All suffering is born within ourselves. Our own hearts are the factories that create suffering. So, what exactly causes suffering in the heart? What is it in our existence that creates suffering in the first place?

What we call "I" is called "the ego."

> **The ego is an absolutely ineradicable emotion based on instinct. It is the belief that the most respected and most important being in this world is none other than "me."**

This is true not only for humans, but for all living things.

The source of suffering is not others, but your own heart.

When the most important existence, "I," is threatened, hurt or falls into some kind of critical situation, we instinctively try to protect it. This defense mechanism is called the "ego," and this is the "I" that we recognize, and the "ego" that causes suffering.

Do We Really Hate Ourselves?

We unconsciously cherish ourselves more than we realize.

"I really hate myself."

"I hate myself so much I want to die."

Even people who hold such thoughts are no exception. In fact, the intense impulse to end one's own life is driven by a powerful ego—essentially, a deep love for oneself. It can even be said that expressing a desire to die is a way of demonstrating this. At its core, it may be a reaction to the frustration of not having "the self that I love and that deserves to be cherished" acknowledged by others.

For example, let's say there was a girl who tried to kill herself after being dumped by her boyfriend. This is not because of the boyfriend himself, but because she cannot forgive the fact that the "I" who should be most valued has been abandoned. In other words, because she loves herself, she cannot accept the reality that she has been ignored. She is causing herself pain with her strong ego, which rebels against things not going her way.

Everyone has the delusion that they should always be treated with the utmost respect.

We think that we should be loved more than anyone else, that we should be accepted, and that our opinions and thoughts should be recognized. The more this delusion grows, the more specific the content becomes, the more energy it generates, and the reaction to the fact that we have not been valued grows disproportionately stronger.

Everyone Thinks "I" Am the Most Important

In both fiction and real life, incidents of death and injury caused by romantic entanglements are not unusual. These are what we often refer to as crimes of passion. A person may come to hate someone they once loved so much that they feel the urge to kill them—or, as in the earlier example, feel such despair that they want to erase their own existence. Whether it's homicide or suicide, both are acts of taking a life. The only difference is whether the target is another person or yourself.

When we fail at something, go through a break up, or reality unfolds differently from what we expected—or rather, from the fantasies we created—that's when anger or sadness arise. The ego is a defense mechanism that operates unconsciously. It is important to understand this "ego" that everyone has, and the strength of its energy.

No matter how much training you do, no one can completely eliminate the "ego" like the Buddha. Just as you think of yourself as important, the other person also thinks of themselves as important. If you are aware of this, you will naturally develop empathy and compassion for others.

> **I want you to think about how you would feel if you were in the other person's shoes, rather than just putting your own interests first.**

In the previous section, we looked at the self-defense instinct, or "ego," as a major factor in causing suffering. This is not the only major factor. The next most common reason is "the urge to compare oneself with others." In Buddhism, this mental state is called *mada*, or "pride."

If we look closely at pride, we can divide it into many patterns, but I will not go into too much detail. It is enough if you know that it can be divided into the following three main categories:

- **The pride of thinking that you are better than another person**

- **The pride of thinking that you and another person are about the same**

- **The pride of thinking that you are inferior to another person**

Ever since humans began living in groups as social animals, we have all been aware of this in our daily lives. It would be better to say that our minds are unconsciously controlled by this way of thinking, rather than that we are aware of it.

If you're on your own, you only have to think about yourself, but when you form a group, you naturally start to take other people into account. Is there anyone in the group who might do something that would be to your detriment? Is there anyone who does anything that disrupts the order of the group?

These kinds of things start to bother you, and you start to check the behavior of other people and compare it to your own. This is where "pride" comes from. And this emotional

The desire to compare is the root of all suffering.

turmoil is the source of painful emotions such as envy, jealousy and contempt, which we will discuss in more detail on the following pages.

No One Can Stop Comparing

Some people may think that they don't care about other people or what they think. When you look at specific examples of pride, however, you will find that you have experienced some of them to a greater or lesser extent.

When you're walking around town and pass someone around your age, you may find yourself almost unconsciously comparing whether they look better than you, have better or worse taste, or are more stylish than you. They're taller, shorter, the same height as you. They are good-looking, not as good-looking, as good-looking as you. If you are self-conscious about your hair, you may think that your hair is thinner, thicker or the same thickness as theirs. If you are concerned about your body shape, you think about whether you are thinner, fatter or the same weight as them. In this way, humans are creatures who cannot stop comparing themselves to others in all sorts of ways. The same is true for parents with children.

"My child is cuter, and smarter, too."

"My child is better at sport than that kid."

We're all thinking the same thing in our hearts. The same goes for old friends who meet again after a long time at a class reunion or a wedding.

"Where did you end up working?"

"So he's still single, huh?"

It is not uncommon for people to compare themselves to others by asking questions like this. When company presidents gather, it often turns into a subtle game of probing each other about the size of their businesses or annual revenue. If writers and editors get together, they can't help but wonder about the success of books that the other has published. When YouTubers get together, the topic of conversation is always the number of channel subscribers and the total number of views of their videos. People are full of pride twenty-four hours a day.

Pride Creates Negative Emotions

I was once full of pride too. When I was a student, I did karate, and I would always look at other men and compare myself to them. I would do this in particular when I used the public bathhouse near Komazawa University, which I attended. As Nihon Sport Science University is located nearby, the public bathhouse was full of athletes with strong bodies.

I would glance at the muscular men sitting next to me as we washed ourselves and think, "Is he stronger than me? Is he weaker than me?" I think they were probably doing the same thing, sizing me up. This is a kind of martial artist thing, and is a typical example of pride in the form of conceit.

In this way, we all live our lives comparing ourselves to others. As a result, negative emotions are born, which might express themselves as "I'm envious," "I'm frustrated," "I feel sorry for them," "What an idiot," or "How pathetic," and these negative emotions become the cause of worries and suffering.

> **Since pride is something that works unconsciously, it cannot be completely eliminated. If you realize that you are being controlled by pride you can take steps to stop it.**

In this book, I will teach you the methods and techniques you need to do this. Let's start with what you can do to calm your heart and mind.

Emotions that arise from instincts such as "ego" and "pride" are referred to as "worldly desires" in Buddhism. Here I will explain the three elements that encourage these negative emotions.

If we were to use medicine as an example of something that moves things in a positive direction, then the three elements I am about to talk about work in the exact opposite way—they function as poison. In fact it may be more accurate to call them "deadly poison."

The Buddha identified these three elements as greed, anger and ignorance, and positioned them as the Three Poisons that can ruin not only the human body and mind, but a person's entire life.

In order to smoothly let go of your suffering, you need to understand the mechanisms of greed, anger and ignorance and look at yourself dispassionately. If you don't know the cause of your suffering, you won't be able to deal with it.

Greed, Anger and Ignorance

Greed means "desire." Think of it as the impulse or energy behind wanting something, seeking something, or moving

Greed, anger and ignorance
are known as the
Three Poisons, and they
corrode the heart.

closer to something we like or want near us. It could be anything: a person you like, money, material possessions or social status. Imagine the desired object as the south pole of a magnet—you feel the urge to become the north pole and be drawn toward it with full force. That longing, that pull toward what you want, is what we call "greed."

Anger means "hatred." It is the opposite energy of "greed." Instead of wanting to get closer to something, it's the impulse to push away—to distance yourself from something you dislike. If the object of your anger is the south pole of a magnet, you also want to be the south pole. If it's the north pole, you want to be the north pole. This is the feeling of "anger"— you hate something, so you want to push it away. But when you can't—when it won't leave—that frustration turns into anger. This is the flow of that process.

Ignorance means "delusion." Because you are ignorant about something, you don't know what to do and become unstable both mentally and physically. Or, because of an inability to act wisely, you end up doing foolish things. If we compare this state of mind to the type of energy we discussed behind "greed" and "anger," it's like being stuck in a loop, spinning round aimlessly with nowhere to go.

The Negative Cycle of the Three Poisons

Although greed, anger and ignorance all posses different characteristics, they are actually closely related.

- **Because greed is not satisfied, anger is born**

- **If anger arises, ignorance prevents us from being able to calm it down**

- **Because of ignorance and a lack of understanding of reality and our own true nature, new greed is born**

We are constantly repeating this cycle.

In modern times, advances in neuroscience have made it possible to scientifically explain human psychological mechanisms to some extent, but the Buddha was already aware of this negative cycle intuitively more than 2,500 years ago.

When you are experiencing the feelings associated with this negative cycle, your heart starts racing and your head starts to feel hot. If this continues, the body becomes exhausted and both the mind and body become unwell. As a result, everything starts to go wrong. So the Buddha used all the evidence he had gained from thoroughly observing the changes in his own body and mind, and the insights he gained became his form of evidence. If left unchecked, suffering will never disappear—it will gradually destroy our body, our mind, and eventually, our entire life—that is why greed, anger and ignorance are the Three Poisons.

This concept may be easier to understand if you think of it in terms of romance.

Suppose there is someone you like. You want to get closer to them. You want to touch them. You want to go out with them. You want to marry them. This is "greed." And you also hope that the other person will come to like you, or at least you hope that they might. But in reality, love is often unrequited. Unfortunately, the desire to "make it happen" is just a convenient delusion created by your heart. Perhaps the other person senses your feelings and avoids you, or you gather up the courage to confess your feelings but are rejected. Then, you will feel anger because the situation isn't going the way you want it to.

It is obvious that the stronger your feelings for the other person, and the greater your heartbreak, the stronger your anger will be. The thought that "the other person might like me too" or "they might fall in love with me" is pure fantasy, and you are essentially wrestling with yourself in a one-sided match. And you end up suffering, consumed by the bubbling anger rising inside you.

What makes it worse is not realizing that all this was just your foolish fantasy. In other words, because of the delusion of ignorance you may find yourself in the same situation again, pursuing another impossible love, or in a worst case scenario, you may even start stalking the person you like.

Likewise, you might get involved with a toxic partner, swear to yourself that you'll never make the same mistake again . . . and then finding yourself falling for exactly the same type of person.

To put it bluntly, we humans are fools, and ignorance is a poison that prevents us from living our lives skillfully.

Blaming Others Will Trap You in Your Suffering

Are you stuck in an endless loop of greed, anger and ignorance? Put your hand on your heart and think about it.

> *"I'm fine. I have no worldly desires and no suffering in life."*

If you can say that with conviction, you are able to live

skillfully without listening to the Buddha's advice, and you don't need this book in the first place. But there are probably not many people like that. Everyone has their problems, big or small. I don't think there are many people who have no problems at all. Most of us need to acquire wisdom so that we can live skillfully.

As I have said many times, the cause of suffering is within ourselves. To see yourself objectively and correctly—this is wisdom. As long as you are unaware that you are viewing yourself through tinted glasses due to "ego" or "pride," your suffering will never end.

> **If you see things in a way that suits you, and think that things will turn out the way you want them to, and then go about things on that basis, you will end up failing, suffering, worrying and building up stress.**

Then, without realizing this fact, you will put the blame on the other person and attack them, saying "It's their fault." And in some cases these stresses can lead to murder or suicide. Human beings are foolish enough to do such extreme things. That is why, in order to avoid this, we need to cultivate the wisdom that will allow us to live skillfully. We need to understand the workings of the human mind so that we can learn to control our emotions.

Buddhism is a systematized methodology for doing this. In chapters 2 to 4 of this book, we will take a closer look at the negative emotions of greed, anger and ignorance. Before learning how to deal with each of these negative emotions, please be sure to keep the main points of this chapter in mind as a fundamental premise.

If you can overcome the wall in your heart, you can let go of your worries.

Is this type of worrying and suffering something that develops in adulthood as we start to become aware of the irrationality of society? No, in my opinion, these feelings can start as early as age three or four. I sense this when I look at the children at the kindergarten in the grounds of the temple where I work, Fukugonji. From a very young age, they start to ask "why?" about many things, and as they learn to speak, they start to vocalize worries and troubles of some kind. As I have said many times, life is a continuous cycle of suffering from birth to death. Suffering is something that we must live with for our entire lives.

If something unpleasant happens, it's easy to end up complaining that someone or something else is to blame. But if you want to be freed from your suffering even a little, you can't just keep blaming everything and everyone else.

"Why do we suffer?"

If you really want to let go of suffering, you have to think seriously about what suffering means—and that is what the Buddha devoted his life to.

What Is the Key to Letting Go of Suffering?

We all live with suffering, but no one would go so far as to take time off work or school to spend some time addressing the issue. But the Buddha dedicated his life to that. He gave up everything in his life to fully confront and examine the suffering of the heart— this is what is called renunciation or leaving worldly life—and it was the path the Buddha chose.

After much thought, he arrived at the Four Noble Truths, his own discoveries. The Four Noble Truths refer to the four sacred truths of "suffering," "cause," "cessation" and "path."

- **Suffering** literally means the suffering we all experience
- **Cause** refers to the different factors and mechanisms that give rise to suffering
- **Cessation** means to recognize the causes of suffering and reduce them
- **Path** refers to the way of letting go of suffering

It may be easier to understand the four truths if you think about them in terms of a product you might see advertised on a television shopping program:

"Cleaning such hard work, isn't it?" (**Suffering**)

"You're busy every day with housework, childcare and work, aren't you?" (**Cause**)

"If the cleaning was done automatically, wouldn't it be a great help?" (**Cessation**)

"Let me introduce you to this product!"(**Path**)

The theory behind the sales tactic used by this sales program is exactly the same as the Four Noble Truths.

- **There is suffering in life**
- **Suffering has a cause**

- **If you know the cause of your suffering, you can reduce it**

- **There is a way to eliminate suffering**

The Buddha deliberately preached in this order so that people would find the four truths easier to understand and relate to.

The Buddha's Conclusion

Nobody likes to suffer, and nobody wants to live with worries. But please bear this in mind:

> **It is not your boss, family, lover or friend that is causing you pain. The delusions in your own mind are the cause.**

So, what exactly should you do to get rid of your suffering? The first step is to look thoroughly within your own heart. If you keep looking for the cause of your suffering outside yourself, you will never be able to see the answers to questions like "Why does it happen?" and "How does it happen?"

As I have been telling you, the causes of suffering lie within ourselves, not outside. In order to get rid of suffering, we need to face our inner selves—our hearts—head-on, but there are various "walls" that stand in our way, such as delusions, preconceptions, greed, anger and ignorance. If you can overcome these inner walls you will be able to let go of your worries and suffering and live with a more peaceful mind.

In Buddhism, focusing attention on your own mind is called "meditation." When you hear the word "meditation," you might get the impression that you have to do something special. But it's not that difficult. I will explain meditation in more detail in Chapter 5, but it is essentially a matter of concentrating and making the most of that energy.

To take it to the extreme, the power of meditation can also be used when you are planning to commit a bank robbery, cheat someone or plotting something else that is harmful. This is a state of being focused in the wrong direction. Buddhist practice, on the other hand, is about directing that same power toward positive self-transformation. Through meditation, the Buddha observed his own mind and discovered profound truths.

If you can understand the causes of suffering and observe the processes that are created in your own mind, you can definitely reduce suffering in your life.

This is the conclusion that the Buddha reached through his training.

How to Break Through the Wall of Anger

"Priest Taigu, what would you do if a complete stranger attacked you for no reason? Would you remain calm and not get angry, because you are a Buddhist monk?"

I often get asked questions like this.

My answer is: "I'll fight. If you hit me once, I'll hit you back twice."

People usually react with surprise: "What? Really?"

Of course, this is a joke, but it is only natural for living things to react by either fighting or fleeing when attacked. In the natural world, if you accept being beaten without putting up a fight, it means death.

Anger is born when the brain judges that you have been attacked or harmed in some way by another person.

This is an emotion that all living things have, and it is necessary for survival—although in modern society, it is not very likely that you will suddenly find yourself face to face with a lion or tiger in a life-threatening situation (although unfortunately, we can't say for sure that the situation described at the top of this page will never happen).

And yet, we often feel irritated and angry in our daily lives. This is because there is a "lion" inside our hearts. We are fighting an invisible enemy because of our own delusions.

Frustration toward others arises from unreasonable expectations.

"I'm angry at my family's attitude."

"My partner cheated on me."

"I can't believe what my boss said to me."

"My celebrity idol was having an affair."

Various situations can make you feel angry, but unless the situation is life-threatening, it is anger that you don't really need to have.

Anger Is Created by Your Own Heart

When you are betrayed by your lover or partner, the anger you feel is not caused by the person who betrayed you. It is caused by your own mind, as a result of your feelings of betrayal and loss.

Let's look at another example. A celebrity you have always been a fan of has an affair. Even though you've never met or spoken to the celebrity in question, you've created an image in your mind of them as being pure and serious, and when that image is shattered, it feels as though you were attacked, and anger rises in response.

The reason you feel betrayed and think you have suffered a loss is because you made the mistake of assuming that the person in question would not betray you or cause you any loss; in other words, you were deluding yourself.

When we feel that our own values, past memories, beliefs,

thoughts or expectations have been denied—this is the true source of anger in the human heart.

As living creatures, we cannot completely rid ourselves of anger, and as I mentioned earlier, there is also "necessary anger" as a survival instinct. However, if we are controlled by delusional anger, it could lead to mental and physical illness. Therefore, we need to train ourselves not to get too caught up in unnecessary anger.

It's Normal for Life Not to Go the Way You Want

Anger is like a fire that starts in your heart. If you leave it unattended, the blazing flames will only grow bigger, and it will become impossible to put them out. It's important to take precautions to prevent fires from starting, and to extinguish them quickly when they do.

> **As a basic premise, keep in mind that life rarely goes the way you want it to and that other people won't be the way you want them to be.**

This is the best way to prevent unnecessary anger.

> *"My family, friends, lover and colleagues should understand my feelings."*

> *"I've done so much for them—they should give me something in return."*

Try not to make convenient expectations of others like this. You will only feel disappointed and angry when what you hope for doesn't happen.

I'm not saying that I'm encouraging negative thinking, but I feel that recently there are more and more people who are too focused on pursuing ideals and only see the bright side of the world. But life is not that simple. What I want to emphasize is: don't fall too far into a mindset of excessive optimism, where you interpret everything in a way that suits your own convenience.

Even so, we are human, and there will be times when we get angry. If you feel anger building, it is very important to put out the fire quickly while it is still small. A fire will not spread unless there is oxygen and dry, flammable material. You can put a small fire out in no time. The same is true of anger. Even if you lose your temper for a moment and a fire is lit, it won't last long unless you throw in some fuel. So, let's create that kind of situation for ourselves.

- **If the cause of anger is an object, move it away**

- **If the cause of anger is a person, leave the area**

These are the best methods of managing our anger effectively.

Don't Throw Fuel on the Fire of Anger

Let's say a married couple have a disagreement and end up arguing. They are both angry with each other and won't back down. And the tit for tat that ensues fuels the anger.

"You didn't put today's laundry in the laundry basket."

"You didn't put the trash out properly."

"The way you wash the dishes is so sloppy."

Words like these are thrown in as fuel, and what should have been a small fire ends up becoming a huge inferno. When this happens, the goal becomes to win the argument or somehow get the other person to admit that you are right, and you end up searching for as much material as you can to throw on the fire. It is truly a fruitless conflict.

The important thing here is to realize that you are in a state of adding fuel yourself. Once you realize this, the first thing to do is to remove yourself from the situation.

Even if your partner accuses you of running away, ignore them, resist the urge to say something back, and get out of there at once.

Then, when you move to a place where there are no other people, take a deep breath. You will then be able to regain your composure, as if the person who was so agitated a moment ago didn't even exist. The same is true for the other person.

If you just stop feeding the fire, the flames of anger will subside.

Separate Mind and Body through Simple Tasks

Moving your body is also an effective way of distancing yourself from anger, and I recommend cleaning or tidying up. Even if you've moved away from the source of anger, if you stay in your room by yourself and just sit there, you'll start thinking things like, "But wait a minute, that definitely wasn't my fault," and the fueling of the fire will start up again. When this happens, there is no opponent, so it's a completely one-sided match. To stop this from happening, try concentrating on cleaning and tidying up methodically: go after that dust that has accumulated in the corners of the room and on your desk, or sort out your clothes.

This separates your mind from your body, helping you calm down without overthinking things. And you're actually making your house cleaner and tidier, so it's killing two birds with one stone. If you're at work, I recommend switching to routine tasks that don't require much thought. Also, touching water can help calm the mind, so try holding your hands under running water, or take a warm bath.

Some people think that getting angry is a bad thing, so they force themselves to suppress feelings of anger. But this is like trying to put out a fire that's already started by just wishing it wouldn't burn, so it's not actually very effective. As I mentioned at the beginning of this chapter, anger is an instinct, so it cannot be eliminated. Instead, being aware of preventative measures and putting out fires at an early stage will bring about good results for both you and the other person. Whether it's a family member, partner, friend, colleague, boss or subordinate, or a celebrity you admire—no matter who it is, they won't always do what you want or what you think is ideal.

> **When you feel angry, take a step back and remind yourself that the anger comes from your own delusions or is because you have created expectations that are convenient for you. And if you end up in a fight with someone, don't throw fuel that will only make the fire spread, but instead, leave the scene and calm down.**

This is the secret to not letting anger consume your heart.

Are you making the people you dislike "gigantic" in your imagination?

Anger Is a Monster

If the emotion of anger grows bigger due to delusions, it will turn into hatred or resentment. Hatred is a feeling of not being able to bear that a certain person exists, and resentment is a feeling that arises when you feel you've suffered some kind of disadvantage due to another person's actions.

As I mentioned earlier, anger is not an emotion that lasts for long periods of time. If you don't keep feeding it, it will naturally subside and you'll wonder why you were so angry in the first place. You could say that "time heals all wounds." This is not the case with hatred and resentment. If you keep adding fuel to the fire of hatred and resentment, it will continue to grow until it gets to a point where you won't be able to extinguish it on your own, and it will have a negative effect on your mental and physical health.

Also, if your emotions overflow in a distorted way, it can lead to bullying, harassment, stalking or other forms of harm to others. Hatred and resentment are like huge monsters that are fueled by anger. So even if you feel the smallest spark of anger, you shouldn't ignore it. Think of it as an emergency alert that is sounding in your heart, saying "Danger!"

Hatred Will Only Cause You to Lose

Anger is an emotion that is instinctively part of being human, and so it is sometimes essential, and we cannot get rid of this emotion completely. Hatred and resentment are different, however.

> **Hatred and resentment are emotions that are completely unnecessary for human life, and**

there is nothing good about having them. You will only lose out by having these unpleasant feelings inside you.

Perhaps you get angry because something unpleasant happens. This is something that can't be helped. But you may find yourself pondering all the reasons you dislike this unpleasant thing that happened.

For example, let's say there is someone at work who you just can't get along with. Even if you only feel that they are a little bit unpleasant at first, you might start to build on these thoughts. You might start thinking "they seem cold toward me" or "did they deliberately look away when we passed each other just now," and you might start to connect all these things together and let your feelings of dislike grow. In other words, you might find yourself using your imagination to the fullest to amplify your dislike.

We are human, so it is inevitable that we have likes and dislikes. That said, you should not let your feelings grow to the point where you hate the other person. This is because you will create delusions in order to keep feeding the feeling of dislike. And although your own delusions will continue to grow, the other person has no idea what is going on inside you, so hating them in this way is pointless and will not change anything.

There is also a possibility that the negative aura you give off will cause people to avoid you or keep their distance. Hatred and resentment are states in which the feeling of anger continues to burn within you, causing inflammation and forming a lump like a cancer cell. In other words, it is like having a malignant tumor growing in your heart. It goes without saying that this is not good for your health.

No matter how unforgivable you think something is, the other person is unlikely to change themselves based on your feelings. Delusions that you create on your own will have to be dealt with by you, on your own. No one else can remove the continually growing tumor in your heart.

Overwrite Your Heart with Good Things

In order to prevent your heart from being controlled by hatred and resentment, it is important to think clearly about the difference between facts and delusions and to set them apart. You must understand that hatred and resentment are emotions you don't need, and you must learn how to overcome them. Of course, they won't just disappear when you understand them. These emotions are deep-rooted.

So, what can you do to get your heart back, when it has been taken over in this way?

> **Everything comes down to overwriting your heart with good things and upgrading it.**

As I will discuss in more detail in Chapter 5, it is important to cultivate what Buddhism calls "positive mental factors"—a kind of fundamental healing that is necessary for true emotional recovery.

Let me talk a little more about resentment. I often receive consultations from people who have been abused by their parents. Even if the parents have already passed away, it is often the case that the children say that they still cannot forgive them.

But parents, too, are human beings—often clumsy, imperfect and foolish. If we look at the question of what made a particular parent abusive, we may be able to sympathize with their upbringing or bad luck in life, but from the perspective of the person who was abused, the only thing they can do is accept the facts as they are with rationality and work on rewriting the negative mental factors that fill their hearts.

For the children of the abusive parents who have passed on, the person they want an apology from is no longer in this world.

"Go to their grave and get everything out of your system," is something I often say to them, advising them to express their feelings out loud at the graveside. I believe that by putting your feelings into words, you can look at your emotions objectively and think about them rationally.

Those who have experienced abuse often imagine an ideal version of a parent, thinking, "If I had been brought up by better parents, I wouldn't have turned out this way." But it's probably true to say that everyone grows up with some kind of dissatisfaction with their parents, to a greater or lesser extent. Also, when you find yourself in the position of being a parent, you will realize how difficult it is. In any case, you must never allow yourself to justify your hatred or resentment. From my own experience, I can say with certainty that it never leads to anything good. Please bear in mind that ultimately, you are the only one who will suffer.

You can never be happy while hating or resenting someone. It is impossible to say, "I hate that person, but I am peaceful and happy."

Are You Fixated on Unnecessary Disgust?

Like hatred and resentment, the emotion of disgust exists as an extension of anger. It is a type of emotion that makes us want to reject or distance ourselves from a certain object. But within this emotion of disgust, there are things that are unavoidable and things that should be let go.

For example, let's say a snake or centipede suddenly appears in front of you. While a few reptile and insect lovers may be interested, most people will be startled and then think, "Ugh, I hate it." This is the moment when feelings of disgust and wanting to keep your distance naturally arise.

This kind of disgust is necessary. Some snakes and centipedes are poisonous, so this is a correct reaction when it comes to protecting yourself from external threats. The human body is designed so that sensors in the brain can detect such threats. It's a survival mechanism, so it's not something we can consciously let go of. But feelings of aversion toward other people are usually unnecessary.

It is probably best to get rid of any other feelings of disgust, especially those you have for other people, as soon as possible.

This type of disgust is not a physiological thing, but something that has come about as a result of the increasing socialization of humans and the development of the brain. It serves no practical purpose, and it will only weigh down your heart.

"That guy is such a jerk."

"I don't really get that person at all."

"People from [insert foreign country here] have no common sense at all."

Stop making unnecessary judgments about what you like and dislike.

You may have thoughts like these from time to time, but stop yourself from letting this type of disgust grow any further within you. This is because, just as each person has a different personality, it is only natural that they also have different values. Other cultures and your culture are not the same, and if you have different attributes or positions, such as being male or female, or being of the same generation or a different generation, your way of thinking will naturally differ.

Our own values and ideas are not the only correct way of looking at things. We cannot impose our own standards on others, and even if we did, it would not change them. This applies to everyone: parents, siblings, teachers, friends, lovers, colleagues, superiors, subordinates, celebrities and the media.

There is no point in making judgments of like or dislike based on the fact that "they are different from me" or "I don't get along with them." In fact, it will only increase the weight of dislike in your heart.

It is enough to recognize the fact that "that person and I are different in this way," and there is no need to make a binary judgment of like or dislike.

Increase the Things You Like

If you feel a sense of disgust toward someone, try to get into the habit of thinking whether that emotion is necessary or not. If you feel aversion to things that could endanger your life, you can be sure that your feelings are correct.

But if you feel disgust toward something that does not threaten your life or well-being, you

should consider it to be just your own misconception or delusion.

Yours is a "unique standard" that has been formed and imprinted on you by your upbringing and environment, and you should not expect others to be the same as you.

By trying to distinguish between necessary and unnecessary forms of disgust, you will develop greater awareness and discernment. And sometimes you may even come to see a new side to something you thought you didn't like. You might suddenly discover that a person you had no time for is more interesting than you at first thought. If you can get to that point, that's a major breakthrough. It's proof that you've succeeded in turning a negative emotion into a positive one.

As long as you continue to reject things you don't like, the world will not open up to you, and your heart will remain in pain.

By accepting things instead, you open yourself up to new possibilities, and your heart will feel lighter as a result.

Have you ever met someone who, at first glance, seemed unfriendly and scary, but when you got to know them turned out to be a really nice person? I think that everyone has felt that at some point. Please cherish that feeling.

A Lesson In How to Get Rid of Assumptions

When I first started karate, there was a certain upperclassman, M, who I didn't get along with at all. I'm not going to beat around the bush here—I actually really loathed him. All the older students at the dojo were more experienced and skilled than me, so there was no way I could keep up as a beginner. Most of the upperclassmen would hold back when we were sparring. M never did though. As it was sparring, I didn't get beaten up too badly, but he would always leave me completely overwhelmed and defeated. I couldn't stop myself from thinking that he didn't need to go that far—I was only a beginner. I felt that I couldn't forgive him for treating me that way.

Then time passed, and the day of a major national tournament arrived—a match that would mark the end of my competitive career. As soon as the match date was decided, M sent me a long letter in a thick envelope. I was surprised when I read it. It was filled with handwritten notes on my technique, strengths and weaknesses. In addition to this, the letter also contained detailed illustrations and advice on how to fight and pace myself during a match. M had gone through all the videos of my past matches and had done a lot of research and analysis.

I was really surprised by this. I thought that M hated me and had been mean to me for a long time. I am now very grateful to M.

And at the same time, every time I remember this incident, I am acutely aware of the pointlessness of unnecessary disgust.

Again, even if you think you dislike something, if you observe it dispassionately, you may see a different side to it. You will realize that this disgust is something that you have created in your own mind. And a new world will open up. Please aim for this. Acting on unnecessary disgust will never lead to true happiness. Letting it go will allow you to live a far more fulfilling and genuinely happy life.

Jealousy of others' success will damage your heart.

Jealousy Is a Strong Anger toward Others

There are times when we feel envious or jealous of others.

> *"The person I like ended up dating someone else."*
>
> *"At work, the young, pretty colleague gets all the attention."*
>
> *"My friends are posting lots of fun things on social media."*

In cases like these, you may feel envious or jealous of someone else. This may come as a surprise, but in Buddhism, jealousy is classified in the "anger" group. While envying the other person, you also feel a strong anger at the fact that other people are happy. So the above complaints really mean: you want to have the person you like for yourself; you want to be liked by those around you and treated better; and you want a more filling and enjoyable life than others.

These feelings stem from greed, the result of your desire to get closer to something or obtain something. The people you like, or your workmates, are showing their affection for or interest in someone else, not you; and your friends and acquaintances seem to be living happier lives than you, so you end up feeling angry, unable to stand this situation.

One of the main characteristics of jealousy is that it is a complex mix of emotions, including not just anger but also fear, resentment and insecurity.

When it comes to romance, you may have had the experience of being hit by an indescribable feeling like "I like you, but I hate you" or "I hate you, but I like you." This is a state of confusion, where various emotions are jumbled together. Even adults, who are supposed to have intelligence and reason, can become confused and lash out at the other person, sometimes attacking them both physically and psychologically. Jealousy is a very troublesome emotion.

Some poisons that are said to cloud the mind can be easily suppressed, while others are more difficult to deal with. Of these, jealousy ranks among the most difficult. It is also considered a difficult emotion to deal with in Buddhism.

Instinctive Jealousy and Social Jealousy

Jealousy is not a simple structure because at one level it shows your interest in another person.

> *"What are you doing now?"*
>
> *"Where have you been?"*
>
> *"Can I see your phone history?"*

But no matter how well-established your relationship is, if you're constantly asking your partner these sorts of questions, they're likely to get fed up.

Let's look at another example. What if you stay out all night without calling home to let your partner know where you are? And when you get home and truthfully explain that you've been out drinking with people from the office, your partner responds with a curt "Oh, really?" If they don't seem jealous or even interested, you might feel a little sad and wonder if they love you. Wanting your partner to be a little jealous but not too jealous is a tricky emotion, unique to humans.

Jealousy can be divided into two kinds: the kind you can let go of, and the kind you can't. If your partner is having an affair, an animal instinct makes you scared that your partner will be taken away from you, and jealousy is a natural response. On the other hand, the trickier kind of jealousy for humans is the one that doesn't stem from instinct or biological drives:

> *"My work colleague is getting promoted faster than me, even though we joined the company at the same time."*

> *"My friend's life is more glamorous than mine."*

> *"The family next door has several expensive cars."*

These feelings are not animal jealousy. They're a form of jealousy that arises from the combination of knowledge and information we've accumulated throughout our lives. It is a reflection of the values and ideas that society has instilled in us—that living a certain kind of life is a marker of "success"—and it could be said that this is an illusion.

In short, the type of jealousy illustrated in the comments above is born from comparing ourselves with others. It's the kind of emotion that emerges precisely because humans are social creatures.

The Opposite of Jealousy is Joy

> *"I hate myself for being jealous of others so easily."*

In this day and age, with social media giving us a full view of other people's lives and activities, it's no wonder that many people end up feeling unnecessary jealousy. The truth is that the solution to jealousy is quite simple.

When you see someone else happy, you should also be happy for them.

This is the most effective thing to do. For example, while watching the Olympics, we cheer on the athletes, saying "Go for it!" Even though they are complete strangers, when they win a gold medal, everyone applauds, says how great they are,and is happy for their success.

In Buddhism, the opposite of jealousy is joy, and the Buddha taught that we should practice being truly happy for others.

Jealousy is a form of anger—one of the inner poisons. If you hold on to it for too long, it will damage your heart.

Everyone has a competitive streak though, and it's easier to simply envy someone rather than be happy for them. It's not so difficult to be happy for someone you don't know at all, or someone who is at a different level to you and you think you can't compete with, but if it's someone you know or someone you think is at a similar level to you, you end up feeling jealous. There are probably very few people who feel jealous of professional athletes or world famous rock stars. When it comes to your own teammates, colleagues or friends, however, you can't help but feel jealous of their successes. Feeling happy for those people is something that we must consciously practice.

Rejoicing in Others' Success Brings Happiness

Professional golfer Tiger Woods is said to cheer for his opponents in the same tournament, calling out words of encouragement. Most people would be more likely to silently urge their opponents in a sporting competition to do badly. But Woods is said to believe that he didn't want an image of a player missing a shot in his own brain, as any negative image, even of a rival doing badly, would have a negative effect on him. Therefore he is happy for the success of others as a matter of course. This kind of attitude creates a positive cycle—when it is his turn to play it will be easier for him to imagine success rather than failure. Understanding this principle helps us recognize the importance of celebrating the success of others.

I have a story I would like to share, based on something that happened to me.

As well as being a Buddhist monk, I am also a karate practitioner. At my dojo there was a junior student, Y, who took sixteen years to earn his black belt. The time it takes to get a black belt depends on the martial arts school, but in the organization I belong to, you can usually get one after about eight to ten years. Y was such a good-natured person that he would put his own match on hold to help his friends with their warm-ups and hitting practice—to the point where he would sometimes forget about his own match. And even though his colleagues and juniors were quickly overtaking him, he was someone who never showed feelings of envy, but instead was genuinely happy for their success.

Although he had never achieved good results in tournaments, everyone at the dojo wanted Y to get his black belt; they felt he truly deserved it.

But here was no leniency in the black belt promotion exams. He was no match for his seniors in the actual fights, and he was defeated again and again. Even so, his fighting spirit never wavered, and finally he made it through the black belt exam in his sixteenth year of practicing.

At a young age Y had been a victim of bullying, so he joined a karate dojo in the hope of becoming stronger. When he finally got his black belt, he cried with happiness, and his fellow dojo members were also overjoyed. Even though he was struggling to win matches and was being overtaken by his juniors, Y was always someone who could rejoice in the success of others. That's why I think he was liked by everyone around him and supported wholeheartedly.

Determine What You Really Want

Feeling happiness at the success of others is really a difficult skill to master, so let me give you some further advice.

One way of avoiding jealousy of others is to create human relationships that don't involve competition. If you connect with someone who is a lot older or younger than you, or someone from a completely different industry, or someone with a different life path, you will probably be able to get on with them quite well, as there is not much to compare or compete over.

Also remember that it's natural to wish you could be more like another person—there's nothing wrong with that in itself. It's important, however, not to let negative thoughts start to seep in, such as thinking it's not fair that that person is always so successful, or that you're better than that person, so why aren't these good things happening to you too?

"Wow, good for them. I'd better work hard too."

If you can learn to observe things in a detached way, separating yourself from the situation and switching your perspective, you will be less likely to get caught up in painful feelings.

It's also a good idea to ask yourself whether something that you think is desirable is really what you're looking for.

For example, there are people who seem to have a great social life, going out with friends every day; and there are people who love to fill their lives with expensive brand-name goods. Don't be misled by the values of a society where people who have lots of friends are regarded in some way superior, or where people who possess lots of brand-name goods are considered successful. If you think carefully about what you really want for yourself, you might realize you enjoy spending time alone in peace, or you might prefer to look for clothes and household items that you really like rather than expensive brand-name goods.

If you look into your own heart and think about what you really want to cherish, you will realize that the painful feelings of jealousy were actually an illusion.

Strong Anger toward Yourself Leads to Regret

"I wish I could go back and do things differently."

"Why did I do that? I shouldn't have done it."

Sometimes dwelling on the past can make us feel depressed. We may experience two kinds of regret: regret for things we did and regret for things we didn't do, but at the root of it all is anger toward ourselves. Regret is also an emotion that belongs to the anger group.

Regret is a feeling that is unique to humans because we have good memories and are able to remember past events clearly. It's probably not an emotion that animals experience. When I look at the dogs and goats we keep at our temple, I can't imagine that they harbor any feelings of regret about a mistake they made years ago.

Humans use their brains in a very sophisticated way, and this allows us to imagine what might have happened if we had done things differently at a certain point in the past. This is why we feel regret. But, as is obvious, no matter how much you regret something, you can't change the past. We only have the present, and we can only carry out actions in the here and now.

If you continue to hold on to feelings of regret, it can lead to a decline in your judgment and performance.

By becoming too attached to the past—which you don't need to think about—you could be negatively affecting the present.

If you regret a mistake you made at work and keep thinking "Why did I do that?" it will make you less efficient and productive at your next task.

Let's switch our mindset to "I'll be careful not to make the same mistake next time" and give our all to the task at hand.

Regret Is a Form of Self-harm for the Heart

You can reflect on the events of the past but there is nothing to be gained in regretting them—these are the teachings of the Buddha.

Regretting that you didn't do something in the right way or that you did something you shouldn't have done is like stabbing yourself in the heart. You are deliberately forcing yourself to experience once more the unpleasant feelings you had in the past.

To keep regretting the same mistake over and over is like stabbing yourself over and over again.

Even if you've gone through a period of a year or two where you manage to forget the mistakes of the past, the memories can still come back, and you'll end up scarred and traumatized. Spending time regretting the past is a form of emotional self-harm—you are hurting yourself.

It's only natural to feel regret, but it's important to not just feel sorry for yourself, but to calmly analyze why you did or didn't do something, and to try to use what happened as a lesson for the future. This is not regret, but reflection, as recommended by the Buddha.

If you're able to intentionally enjoy your regrets, saying things like, "Man, I was such a kid back then. What was I even thinking? Youthful mistakes can be scary, huh?"—that's perfectly fine. If you can turn your past actions or feelings into a story you can laugh about, either to yourself or with others, it shows that you've gained the ability to look at those moments objectively. If you're able to turn what used to be your "dark history" into a lighthearted topic, then recalling it no longer causes emotional pain. In the end, what matters most is how you choose to interpret what happened in the past — how you think about it, and how you process it within yourself.

Blaming Someone Else Won't Relieve the Pain

Be aware that you yourself chose to do the thing in the past that you regret. It's easy to blame others.

> *"I went to that school because my parents said it was the better option."*
>
> *"If I hadn't trusted what X said, I'd never have got into that terrible situation."*

> **No matter what the relationship with the other person is, or what kind of advice is given, it is ultimately you yourself who takes action.**

It is you who makes the decision. Don't shift the blame onto others. Reflect on your mistake honestly, and vow to yourself that you will not make the same mistake again. And to ensure that you don't end up blaming others or something else later on—when you are about to act or make a decision, ask yourself if this is really what you want to do. If your answer to yourself is yes, then go ahead and do it.

Facing up to yourself and thinking for yourself takes strength. It's hard work. We often tend to make decisions based on what other people say. It's much easier that way. But in order to live a life without regrets, you must never give up on thinking for yourself.

If you have thought things through thoroughly and made your own decision, you can accept whatever the outcome is knowing that this is a result of a choice you made. You may not be able to eliminate regret completely, but you can reduce its frequency.

> **One way of eliminating regret is to change your evaluation of what has happened.**

When I was a child, I once got seriously injured because I didn't listen to my mother. She had told me not to change my clothes in front of the stove because it was dangerous. But one day, when my parents were out, I started to do exactly what she'd told me not to. My younger sister tried to copy me, somehow we ended up having a fight, and finally I knocked the kettle off the stove, badly burning my foot. I had to undergo surgery many times, and at one point I even ended up in a wheelchair. I still have the scars to this day.

At the time, this incident was a huge shock for me. I was filled with regret and guilt for not following my parents' instructions. But as I grew up, I came to think of this incident as a warning to myself. Now, every time I look at my scar, I am able to remind myself not to get carried away by surrounding circumstances. I remember that doing something you know you shouldn't do always has consequences. So this wound is a blessing that prevents me from repeating mistakes I made in the past.

It may take some time for you to be able to think this way. But I hope you can try to change the way you look at things and the way you evaluate those things and that in doing so, you can say goodbye to regret.

The secret to a life without regrets is to "dig your own grave early."

While You're Alive, Dig Your Own Grave

One of life's ultimate regrets is to find yourself on your deathbed, wishing you'd done something, or that you'd told someone how you felt. A similar situation is wishing you had done something for a person who has now passed away. This last regret in particular is hard to recover from. That's why I believe it's best to experience plenty of regret while you're still young, and use those experiences to develop the skill of letting go.

It's okay to make mistakes. It's good to reflect on your mistakes. But it's not good to regret them. Let's be very aware of this from now on. As long as you are alive and well, you can make amends if you feel you need to. "There's always tomorrow" is a valid way of thinking.

Obviously, however, you never know when you—or someone close to you—might die.

> **So in order to live a life without regrets, don't put off dealing with the things that are bothering you right now, and face them head on as they come up.**

"Dig your own grave early," was a phrase one of my masters liked to use. These words usually relate to bringing some kind of ruin upon yourself, but the sense in which my master used them was different. He meant that if you dig your own grave before you die, you will be able to live a happy life. He wasn't talking about spiritual forces or anything mystical:

> **When you become aware of death, you will be aware that the grave is waiting for you, and you**

will be determined to live each day to the fullest without wasting the time you have left.

When I first heard this, I was a little confused, but now I understand its truth and realize that it is exactly right. Digging your own grave while you're alive becomes a powerful act that supports a life free of regret. So, please make decisions as if you were going to die tomorrow, and try to be fully aware of living today to the fullest. If you do, I believe you'll find yourself regretting far fewer of your actions and words than you do now.

Sadness Is Actually a Form of Anger

This may come as a surprise, but the emotion of sadness is included in the Buddhist concept of *dosa*, meaning "ill will," a group of emotions that includes anger. If you are experiencing sadness, you might describe the feeling as your heart aching. In other words, it is as if your heart is being attacked in some way, or that something that you once had is lost.

It follows a mechanism similar to physical pain—someone hits you, you feel physical hurt, and this gives rise to anger. That's why sadness and anger are treated as part of the same emotional group.

For example, if conflict between people escalates into a fight, some people might get angry and fight back, while others might start crying with sadness. The same event can make you angry or sad, depending on the situation and your personality. That's why the emotions are grouped together. We feel sadness in the prefrontal area of the brain, which is responsible for controlling memory and emotions. The human brain is highly developed and excels at memory, so it is difficult to forget sad events that have happened in the past. That is why we shed tears when we remember people who have died or parted ways with us many years ago.

It is said that animals, like humans, can feel sadness about things that happen right in front of them. But humans have greater memory and imagination, and the human brain amplifies feelings of sadness by drawing on the things we have heard, read and experienced in the past.

Because of our overactive imaginations, we sometimes feel sad about the future that lies ahead too. For example, what if one of your parents became ill and the doctor told you they had only six months to live? Even though they are still alive in front of you, you imagine what will happen in six months' time, and you become disheartened, sad, and tears start to well up.

This type of a reaction is a privilege granted only to humans, but it is also causes suffering. Other animals probably don't imagine the future and become sad.

All Worldly Things Are Transitory

When we experience intense sadness, we often lose the ability to see our own hearts objectively. For example, everyone knows that all living beings eventually die. But when a close friend is close to death or a pet becomes seriously ill, we suddenly lose our objectivity and are unable to face up to the facts.

As the sadness grows, our egos, or our own beliefs, begin to waver. Our delusions and preconceptions come into play. Because we mistakenly think that our parents will always be there to protect us, and that our love for our partner will last forever, the sadness we feel when we lose them is great.

Practice putting aside
your feelings
of sadness.

The stronger those beliefs and expectations are, the more intense the grief becomes when they are shaken or broken. When we calm down and look at ourselves objectively, we understand that the elderly usually die before us, that most couples eventually part ways, and so on. But despite this, another version of ourselves—the self that refuses to believe it, the self that loses its sense of ego—surfaces and adds fuel to our sadness.

Ultimately, sadness is mostly triggered by separation from someone we deeply care about, or by being hurt or betrayed by someone we trust. In other words, sadness arises when the hopes, wishes and emotional expectations we've built in our hearts are shattered or lost.

I understand how hard it is to accept that certain things are really happening, especially when something or someone close to you is moving away or disappearing from your life. But this is where I'd like you to remember the Buddhist concept of impermanence—the idea that all things are transient.

Everything in this world is temporary and ever-changing and nothing lasts forever.

It's important to always keep this truth in your heart.

If the person you are sad about is a family member, a lover, a close friend or someone else you love and care about, a situation that causes you to part ways will be very distressing. But the degree of sadness you feel will vary greatly depending on whether you were aware that the relationship would end at some point or not. This is one technique for managing the emotion of sadness.

Effective Techniques for Controlling Sadness

Putting your sadness aside for the time being is one method of dealing with grief. For example, if you've just gone through a breakup and then suddenly get transferred to a new department at work, you'll likely find yourself so focused on learning new tasks and building new relationships that you don't even have the time or the emotional space to think about love.

> **We can force ourselves to create situations where we don't have time to be sad, because we have other matters to prioritize.**

Of course, this depends on what's realistically possible for you, but if you are able—changing jobs, moving to a new place, taking a trip, starting a new hobby—these can all help shift you into a mindset of "I have more important things to deal with right now." This allows you to temporarily suppress the sadness in your heart.

Staying in the same place, or remaining in an environment that constantly reminds you of the source of your sadness, is not recommended. Doing so may prevent you from moving forward, leaving you stuck in a prolonged emotional slump.

What is important is to employ reason and look at your emotions objectively. If you think about things logically and act with the understanding that you are taking certain actions of your own free will in order to let go of your pain, I think you will be able to manage your sadness. This is one reason why funerals are good. When someone close to you dies, you feel great sadness, but at the same time you have to contact the people who knew the deceased, arrange for the funeral service, notify the authorities and so on, and you end up in a whirlwind of organizing one thing after another. You're sad but you don't have time to be sad—this situation will continue for a while. Pushing the feeling of sadness to the background while you are busy dealing with all these practicalities is one way to help your sadness fade.

What We See at the End of Our Sadness

One last thing I want to tell you is that you should grieve thoroughly. No matter how strong human emotions are, they are eventually calmed down by the secretion of a hormone in the brain, called serotonin. Of course there are individual differences, but for most people when the emotion of sadness reaches its limit, it will then turn into a positive feeling.

After the Great East Japan Earthquake in March 2011, I visited the disaster area many times as a volunteer. The grief suffered by the victims immediately after the earthquake is unimaginable and beyond description. When I went back there a few years later though, I began to hear a lot of comments like, "There's nothing we can do about it" and "We can't change what's happened, so we'll just have to do our best moving forward."

I think everybody understood that sadness alone does not help you move forward. At some point, reason becomes stronger than emotion, and people start to think logically about recovery, making practical plans for cleaning up this and fixing that. This is the feeling I got from them.

Although sadness is a painful emotion, you should not completely shut your mind off in order to avoid dealing with it. If you do this, your heart will never heal.

The important thing is to be prepared for the fact that the

things and people you love will eventually drift away from you, and to live each day remembering that all things are impermanent. You should also try to control these emotions by facing yourself as objectively as possible, and by taking the time to thoroughly grieve, as well as finding time to put your grief aside for a while. By doing so, you will be able to create a life with less suffering than the one you're living now.

How to Break Through the Wall of Ignorance

Anxiety has several causes. You may feel anxious imagining things that could happen in the future. Other times, even if there is no specific problem, you might feel anxious for a reason you are not quite sure of. Anxiety is a product of two uniquely human abilities that developed as our brains evolved: memory and imagination.

As mentioned in the section on sadness in Chapter 2, the emotions included in the anger group mainly arise from present or past events, whereas anxiety arises when we use our imagination to think about the future.

> **Being able to predict the future and take measures to deal with it is a necessary skill for avoiding danger and surviving.**

Certain types of anxiety can be useful, but there are other types that are pointless. For example, let's say you're about to take some kind of exam. You get anxious about what will happen if you don't pass, so you study really hard. This is a good thing, as it gives you the motivation and energy to work toward your goal.

On the other hand, you may be feeling a vague sense of anxiety about the future, but you don't know what to do about it, and you spend each day feeling listless. This is the kind of anxiety that is pointless.

Vague anxiety can be discarded once you make its true form visible.

When you feel anxious, it is important to clarify exactly what you are anxious about and then to take concrete action to resolve it. If you have feelings of vague anxiety that you can't connect to any concrete action, these feelings serve no benefit other than to make you feel heavy-hearted. If you want to get rid of your anxiety, you need to clarify exactly what is causing it.

The Emotion of Fear in Contemporary Society

A feeling similar to anxiety is fear. Fear can be physical, mental, or both. It can be something that you feel when you encounter something bigger and stronger than you, and you sense that you are in danger of harm or of even losing your life. In this type of situation fear could be described as an animal instinct.

> **Fear is an emotion that is programmed into all living creatures, and is essential for avoiding any kind of crisis.**

In contemporary society, where we hardly ever have to deal with immediate life-threatening dangers, people often experience unnecessary fear—and I feel that this contributes to a sense of difficulty or discomfort in life. For that reason, I would like to emphasize that fear is an emotion we need to pay careful attention to.

For example, you join a company, do your job and earn a salary. Earning a good salary, and having a high level of motivation to earn more seems like a good thing at first glance. But it could also be said that people are driven by a sense of fear that they will lose their source of income, or that they have to make more money. And there are other people who take advantage of these kinds of fears.

This may seem like a big jump, but there are religions that have used these emotions to manipulate their followers, telling them that if they don't do a certain thing then they will go to hell or bad things will happen to them, stoking unnecessary fears.

Even if you think you are acting based on positive emotions like "I'll do my best" or "I'll try my hardest," in reality, there are many cases, especially in modern society, where you are driven by fear or your emotions are being controlled.

Although we are less afraid of physical things like fire, floods or being attacked by wild animals, I feel that a major problem in today's society is that we are increasingly afraid of things we cannot see or that are psychological in nature.

Anxiety Can Become Fear without You Realizing

Although we may do our best not to feel anxious about growing old or dying, it's not that easy. But other animals don't know that they're going to die, and I don't think they feel any anxiety or fear about it.

I doubt that either dogs or cats think, "When will I die?" But because humans feel anxious about the future, they worry about getting sick and save money so that they can have a peaceful retirement. This is another example of a useful type of anxiety, which results in us being able to live life cheerfully and happily. (The other side of the coin here would be not to worry at all about aging and perhaps becoming one of those elderly people who continue driving their car without thinking that their judgment is dulling, and risk running over someone.)

> **The key is not to try to eliminate anxiety entirely, but to face it honestly.**

I'm not saying you should be overly cautious, but you should be aware that there is a certain amount of anxiety that is necessary in order to overcome risks that surround you.

The real danger lies in unnecessary anxiety—the kind that multiplies and spreads until it morphs into fear.

> **When feelings of fear become dominant, reason stops working and it becomes impossible to make the right decisions.**

Nowadays, it's not only dubious religious groups, investment seminars and self-help workshops that routinely use fear as a tool to manipulate people—our governments, mass media and corporations do it too. What started out as a small worry turns into fear as you hear more and more bad news. When people lose the ability to think rationally, that's when others strike—and that's how people end up being deceived.

With things like the COVID pandemic, struggling economies and wars and conflicts around the world, everyone seems to be living with a constant undercurrent of anxiety.

Dealing with Fears and Anxieties

If you're wondering how to regain a sense of balance in the face of fear and anxiety, I recommend meditation.

Set aside some time once a day to reflect on the emotions you are feeling and ask yourself if your worries are really necessary.

Rather than letting yourself be invaded by vague feelings of anxiety, try to visualize the specific content of your unease. It can also be helpful to write down what comes up during meditation in a notebook or journal. With this systematic approach to gathering information about the things that make you anxious, you can then decide what measures to take.

When I first took part in a national karate tournament, I felt like I was going to be crushed by my feelings of anxiety. At that time, the senior students simply advised me to just keep practicing. By facing my own worries and practicing thoroughly, I became more confident and my anxiety naturally decreased.

We may never be able to completely eliminate anxiety, but if we prepare as thoroughly as we can, we can reach a place where we can say, "If it doesn't go well after all this, then that's just how it is," and let go—in a healthy, accepting way.

Another option is to seek advice from counselors or other professionals.

If you can't face your own anxieties or think clearly anymore and you find yourself in a situation where your worries are turning into fear, I recommend that you don't try to manage things on your own, but ask for help from other people. For example, if you are worried about your future finances, you could consult a financial planner, or if you are worried about finding a job or changing jobs, you could talk to a careers counselor.

If there are no specialists or counselors nearby who can listen to you straight away, try talking to a friend or trusted acquaintance. A dispassionate third-party perspective can often help us clear our minds of difficult emotions and help us see our own situation more objectively. Of course the ultimate solution to your problem is something that you have to settle on yourself, but talking to someone else can be an important step on this journey. The stories I share on my YouTube channel are also meant to help people who have lost their calmness to regain their reason. It's like splashing a little cold water on a confused mind, offering gentle suggestions to encourage people to look at their anxiety from a different perspective.

One important point is that it's often better to talk to third parties rather than your own family about problems like these.

The instinct of a family member is often a strong desire to do something to help; it's hard for them to be objective in the face of the suffering of someone who is close to them. You and your family may end up getting caught in a whirlwind of anxiety, unable to make a calm decision.

When we judge a situation, two systems are at work. One is based on intuition using experience, and the other is a decision made using logical thinking. Sometimes intuition is right, and sometimes it's wrong—when you back it up with data, you may find that your assumptions were not as solid as you thought.

In Buddhism, one key teaching is that if we allow ourselves to make emotionally driven decisions based solely on intuition, it often won't lead to the outcomes we desire, and we may fail to make the right choices. That's why using reason and self-awareness is considered essential.

> **The most important thing is not to deny your fears and anxieties, but to accept yourself as you are—emotions and all. You need to be clear about the fact that you are anxious about something, and acknowledge it to yourself.**

After acknowledging this, take a step back and take some time to think about the issue you are worried about calmly, asking yourself if what you perceive is really the case. This is the wisdom of the Buddha, and it will help you deal with difficult situations.

Impatience Lies between Hope and Despair

One emotion similar to anxiety is impatience.

> *"I can't get the results I want at work."*

> *"I can't see a future for myself."*

> *"I really want to get married, but my love life isn't going well."*

> *"My boss suddenly gave me an urgent task to do."*

> *"I'm going to be late for our meeting because of a sudden problem."*

You may find yourself panicking in response to situations

in your daily life that are unexpected or irregular, making you lose your composure and start to panic. Compared to anxiety and fear, impatience could be defined as having hope somewhere in your heart that there is still something you can do about a situation, but at the same time not having a concrete solution for dealing with the problem.

Converting Impatience into Positive Energy

Impatience is a difficult emotion to suppress, especially when you're in a hurry and the situation remains unchanged. That's why we end up causing accidents from panicking, or damaging relationships by taking our frustration out on those around us.

For example, when a train is delayed—perhaps due to a an accident that is not the railway company's fault—some people take out their anger on station staff, even though the workers are doing their best under circumstances beyond their control. This kind of reaction often stems from an inability to find emotional balance, and ultimately, it doesn't make the train move any faster.

There's little benefit to impatience. Those who frequently feel restless and struggle to maintain a calm mindset tend to accumulate more stress than those with a laid-back personality. Impatience itself, however, isn't inherently negative. Instead of suppressing it entirely, it can be helpful to channel it in constructive ways.

In some cases, pressure and urgency can fuel creativity. Many people in creative fields find that looming deadlines push them to come up with brilliant ideas at the last minute. Similarly, moments of crisis can trigger an adrenalin rush, bringing a heightened focus or strength that allows people to perform beyond their normal capacity and navigate difficult situations.

While constantly panicking due to poor preparation isn't ideal, occasional moments of urgency can be beneficial. Instead of fighting impatience, the key is learning how to harness its energy in a positive way.

Decide for Yourself What to Prioritize

That said, if you can, you'll want to let go of this feeling of impatience, too. What can we do to achieve this?

It may not be a quick fix, but ideally, as I mentioned earlier, you should be able to turn your impatience into a positive force by using it to your advantage. And it is important to decide in advance what your priorities are in a situation where you are in a hurry.

> **Even if you are feeling impatient, if you use your rational mind to think objectively about how to act in the situation you are in, the impatience you feel will gradually subside.**

For example, let's say your supervisor at work is the high-pressure type, always rushing you to get work done. Of course that would make anyone feel anxious. But if you can accept that this is a normal part of everyday life, and you can get used to the situation, then you will naturally feel less impatient.

Impatience occurs when your body and mind are in a state of tension. Feeling tense is a sign that your body is telling you to focus on a particular thing. So it's better to think of it as an opportunity to think about and look at something positively.

When you know
your life's priorities,
you won't feel
so impatient.

There are also times when you may feel a more vague sense of impatience:

> *"All my friends are getting married, but I haven't even met anyone yet."*
>
> *"My colleagues are steadily building their careers, but I've been stuck in the same place for years."*
>
> **In this kind of situation, as with the anxiety we discussed earlier, it is necessary to clarify what you are feeling impatient about, what you value most, and to clarify your priorities.**

If you're thinking that you want to get married as soon as possible, it's a good idea to actively seek out places where you can meet new people, or ask your friends to introduce you to someone. But on deeper reflection, you may realize that your impatience was simply influenced by those around you, and that, in reality, you want to focus on your career before marriage.

If you can clarify the source of your impatience and take concrete action in response, the feeling of impatience should naturally disappear. If you remain in a constant state of panic or tension, this creates a heavy psychological burden.

To prevent such a burden from accumulating, it's important not to let yourself be controlled by the emotion of anxiety. Get used to it, make peace with it, use it to your advantage, think things through concretely, and choose actions based on what's most important.

Try putting these ideas into practice, one step at a time.

First of All, Try to Doubt Everything

Let's talk a little more about anxiety and fear. If feelings of anxiety and fear continue to build up inside you, they can lead to distrust, where you find it hard to believe in various things.

As I mentioned in the section on fear, fear is essential for avoiding danger and risk in our daily lives. When primitive humans were threatened by predators and other dangers, having fear and sense of distrust led to cautious behavior, and it was this that enabled us to survive.

In modern times, it is rare for enemies to suddenly appear and attack us, but it is important to be on our guard for things that pose a psychological threat.

Whether in business management or in our personal lives, not everyone in the world has good intentions. There are, unfortunately, individuals who act with malicious intent—those who deceive, manipulate or try to bring others down.

In modern society, things like investment fraud, pyramid schemes or telephone scams where the caller tries to swindle money are rife. This is why having a sense of skepticism is crucial. While the nature of distrust may have changed over time, it remains an essential emotion for human survival.

A Healthy Dose of Distrust

Although some distrust is necessary, people who have too much of it tend to accumulate a great deal of stress.

You will always be on your guard, thinking "I wonder if this person can be trusted?" or "I wonder if they are trying to deceive me?" so you will never be able to relax.

If anxiety and fear become too strong, distrust will only

increase. In other words, it becomes a fear of being harmed or experiencing some kind of loss or disadvantage.

What we need to be careful about is this: if you constantly approach people with a deep sense of distrust, eventually no one will trust you either.

"Is it true?"

"Surely what they're saying can't be right?"

If these are always your thoughts as you look suspiciously at another person, that person will end up not liking you. Having some level of distrust is important. But extreme distrust leads to a paranoid mindset, which not only drains your own mental and physical energy but also makes others lose faith in you and distance themselves.

For example, when you're learning to drive, you are taught how to anticipate dangers, such as a person suddenly appearing on the road in front of you with no warning. Interestingly, this way of teaching aligns closely with Buddhist teaching. You can't drive a car safely without trust. But if you have too much distrust, you will be afraid to drive and won't be able to get going at all.

In Buddhism, the teaching of "constantly observing oneself and practicing self-discipline" is rooted in this idea. If you do not have some level of doubt about yourself, you may become overconfident. On the other hand, if you are excessively distrustful of yourself and those around you, you may find it difficult to move forward with anything. Ultimately, maintaining balance is the most important thing.

Think for Yourself—Check with Those You Trust

If you accept what someone says without any critical thinking or questioning, this is considered "ignorance" in Buddhism—meaning a state of being uninformed or lacking wisdom.

After giving his teachings, the Buddha always told his disciples: "If you have any questions or concerns about what I have just said, do not hesitate to ask."

If no one raised their hand, he would repeat the same question. He would continue to do this until it was clear that everyone had understood and accepted the teaching. What this means is that, no matter who is speaking—even if it is the Buddha himself—you should never accept someone's words blindly. Instead, you are encouraged to question and examine them critically.

Incidentally, even if a person without wisdom thinks hard and comes to what they believe is a rational conclusion, ignorance remains ignorance—this, too, was one of the Buddha's conclusions. The teaching is that "fools should not judge for themselves, but should listen to the words of wise people. Then, they should compare their own answers with the opinions of wise people. If they do not match, they should recognize their own ignorance and question their own thoughts."

This does not mean that you should believe in neither yourself nor in others.

Make sure you surround yourself with people you can trust, people who are good and wise, and be in touch with their opinions on a daily basis. At the same time, you must never neglect to think for yourself and ask yourself whether what they are saying is really correct.

Based on this premise, unnecessary distrust is the feeling of being unable to trust the people you should be able to trust. If a foolish person thinks for themselves, they will stray from the right path without realizing it. Because they didn't consult with the right people—the people they really trusted, they may end up being deceived by someone suspicious.

For example, parents are not necessarily all-powerful, but when there is a problem, they will do their best to help their children. If you lose the ability to trust those who genuinely care about you, then that is truly the end of the road.

> **While distrust is important, if you cannot believe in the things that truly deserve your trust, you will find yourself without any salvation.**

This is why distrust is included in the "ignorance" group—and it's also what makes this emotion so complex and difficult to navigate.

How to Identify Who to Trust

On my YouTube channel *Osho Taigu's One Question & One Answer,* I once received a question asking "Can we trust you, Priest Taigu?" I thought this was fair enough—after all, in this day and age, there are many questionable things, including situations that resemble mind control.

"No, no, please doubt me too."

This was my answer, and it is also the fundamental stance of Buddhist thought. As I mentioned earlier, the Buddha let his disciples ask questions until they had no more. I will accept any questions and any criticism.

If you try to destroy a theory from various angles and

Evaluate people based on their actions, not their words.

still can't, then it may be something that you can accept and believe in. For example, there is one clear difference between education and brainwashing:

Education provides information for the benefit of the learner, while brainwashing conveys information for the benefit of the one delivering it.

Ultimately, it is important to acquire knowledge and experience for yourself and then make your own decisions.

In modern society, values are becoming increasingly diverse, and there is an abundance of mixed information. For this reason, we need to develop a healthy sense of distrust in order to be able to discern what is truly important to us.

Doubt even yourself. And, try to doubt others at least once. After that, you should use your own wisdom to examine things from all angles, choose what you think is the best at that point in time, and believe in it.

If I were to give a concrete method—this comes from the words of the Buddha—it would be this: you should not believe what a person says, but rather look at what they have done and the results they have achieved

People who talk a good game but don't back it up with action are not worth believing.

Some people might ask, "How can a Buddhist monk preach that we should doubt others?"

But that, too, is the Buddha's teaching. I do my best to doubt everything, no matter who says it. If you do this, you will be able to discern those who truly care about you and give you sincere advice, and those who are truly wise.

The End of the World Can Be a New Beginning

There are certain moments in our lives that may fill us with despair.

"I broke up with someone I really loved."

"I lost someone very dear to me."

"I failed the entrance exam."

"I was betrayed by someone I trusted."

When such moments arrive, they leave us feeling despair. Bear in mind that despair does not come out of nowhere. There are several steps, or rather, other negative emotions such as sadness and discouragement that must arise before despair is reached. These emotions come first, and when they become too intense, they escalate into despair.

When faced with despair, the shock can be overwhelming. Some people might think it's the end of the world, or that they just can't go on. They become depressed, lose their energy, stop smiling, refuse to have anything to do with others, and in the worst cases, they may even take their own lives. There are countless instances where despair leads to tragic outcomes.

Despair takes considerable mental toll. It inevitably impacts daily life—work, studies and decision-making all suffer and your judgment will become clouded. Despair means you have lost all hope.

This does not mean there is no hope in despair. On the contrary, you can also look at despair as something positive.

Despair means that you have reached your limit and signifies a point where things cannot get any worse than they are now.

If you can accept that this is the case, then instead of dwelling on the pain of despair, perhaps you can try to shift your perspective:

"It was painful to be disappointed, but what I was hoping for was never within my reach to begin with."

"It was something I didn't need in the first place."

When one path is cut off, it means another path is opening up. The moment we feel despair might be an opportunity, a chance to reassess what truly matters to us.

What You Can See when You Hit Rock Bottom

My Buddhist name is Gensho Taigu, but it used to be Gensho Butsudo. The reason I changed my name was—surprising as it may seem—despair. As a novice monk, I was constantly thinking, "I need to attain enlightenment" and "I have to become a better person." But no matter how hard I trained, I couldn't seem to reach that state of mind. I fell into despair and I wrote a letter to my master saying, "I'm finished."

The letter I received back said:

> Fall! Fall all the way down! You are a great fool, so from today on, you shall be known as "Taigu" [Great Fool].

Reading this made me realize I had never truly acknowledged my own foolishness. In my desperation to become *more* and *better*, I had been clinging greedily to my own desires. Letting go of that struggle allowed me to reset my heart and start anew. That moment became a major turning point in my life.

So now I see things this way:

A mild shock is not fatal, so people will continue to repeat their foolish actions. If you're going to experience a shock, it's better to have one so big that it completely breaks you—because only then can true transformation begin. Therefore, it is better to feel despair as early as possible, while you are still young.

I view this as a completely positive thing. At the temple, I tell my disciples every day, "Hurry up and despair, hurry up and despair." They're all pretty stubborn, though, and it's not easy to get them to give in!

Ultimately, recovering from despair means that you have been able to let go of your own desires. You have experienced this not just as giving up, but as seeing things clearly and moving forward.

This is by no means a bad thing.

Buddhism teaches that it is better to give up all worldly desires. Appetite, sexual desire, lust for power, lust for money. Only by relinquishing these desires, in other words, by letting them go, can you approach enlightenment.

The phrase "to let go" means "to give up," but in Buddhism it also means "to see clearly."

By letting go,
what truly matters
becomes clear.

Try to see clearly whether or not the thing you desire is something you really need. It is about assessing whether your goals are truly achievable and whether they align with your mind, body and abilities. This act is equal to "letting go."

> **If it's something you really need, you won't give up no matter what. If you can give up, it means it wasn't something you really needed.**

It means there is something else—something that is more suited to you—waiting ahead. After despair, only hope remains. Let's do our best to recognize this truth.

If You Can't Let Go, Your Suffering Will Continue

This mindset applies to every stage of life and it can be incredibly powerful. Despair related to school or career choices is a classic example. Consider a student attending a prestigious high school with excellent grades, consistently scoring in the top percentile in mock exams, and earning an 80 percent or higher probability of admission to their dream university. If such a student fails their entrance exam, they often fall into deep despair.

There's nothing wrong with taking the exam again the following year. But if they keep failing year after year—should they not start questioning whether that university was truly necessary for them?

The same goes for those who have "settled" by going to a university that they felt was nothing more than a backup to the school they really wanted to go to. Many in this situation find it difficult to accept the fact that they had to give up on their first choice, and may continue to agonize for the next four years, thinking that this wasn't what they expected or where they felt they should be. In this way, they spend their school days looking down on their classmates without facing reality.

Then, if their job search doesn't go as planned, this "grass is always greener" mentality only worsens, making them constantly crave what they don't have. Let's imagine they had interpreted their failure in the university entrance exam in another way:

> *"I simply wasn't meant to attend my first-choice university"*
>
> *"This is my true ability now, so there's nothing I can do about it."*

If they had been able to look at the situation from this perspective, they might have been able to live a fulfilling campus life with a new attitude, without suffering or having complexes. By "letting go," talents and aptitudes that had not been noticed before may have blossomed, and they may have been able to get a job at the company they wanted.

The same applies to love: even if you are rejected by someone you like and feel despair, don't let it get to you. Think of it as an opportunity to meet someone even more suitable or wonderful.

Most of the people in the world we regard as "successful" have experienced despair at some point in their lives. It is because they realized that there was no hope on one path that they were able to find hope on a different path and walk the road to success. I think that this pattern is far more common than we think.

Japanese comedian Sanma Akashiya once said: "Just being alive is a huge win."

That's absolutely true, and I hope that these positive words can offer hope for people who are feeling despair.

My Mother—Turning Despair into Hope

I hope that you will remember Sanma Akashiya's words when you are confronted with a situation where you have to face death and despair. For example, even if you are diagnosed with cancer and it has progressed to stage 4, and you are told how long you have left to live, you should not lose heart. Receiving such news is undoubtedly a major shock. But even in that moment—you are still alive. It is easy to forget this simple but crucial fact. If you don't find hope in that reality, you won't be able to cherish the time you have left. While you are regretting past lifestyle choices, feeling pain or drowning in sorrow, time continues to move forward. And that is an incredible waste. In order to make the most of your limited time, it is essential to hold onto hope and think, "From this moment forward, I will live without regret."

> *"If there's something you want to do—do it now."*
>
> *"If there's a place you want to visit, go there."*
>
> *"If there's someone you want to apologize to, do it as soon as possible."*

This is what I tell those who are facing illness and an uncertain future.

To give you a personal example, my own mother turned

despair into hope and achieved something of a miracle. During a health check-up about five years ago, she was diagnosed with stage 3 colorectal cancer, and the doctor told her: "There is a possibility that it has metastasized, and because you are of a certain age, even if it were possible to remove it surgically, you might not be able to walk afterward."

At this time, my mother was eighty-two years old. Should she take the risk and undergo surgery, possibly losing her ability to walk? Or should she avoid surgery and live out the rest of her life while receiving treatment? She was faced with a big decision.

"If you tell me to operate, I will. But if metastasis is found, you will need to have another operation. Considering your physical condition, it might be better not to have surgery." This was the doctor's opinion. My mother, however, chose to have the surgery despite the risks, saying, "If I think of myself as already dead, I can do anything."

Perhaps it was because she was able to accept her fate and "let go," she was able to make a bold decision. And my mom won the bet. The surgery was a success, there was no evidence of metastasis, and after enduring the difficult rehabilitation, she was able to return to her normal life. More than five years have passed since then, and she is still walking around in good health.

No one knows what will happen to us in the end. That's why you should choose your own path and live your life without regrets.

Even if my mother had become unable to walk or her cancer had spread and her condition had deteriorated rapidly, I think she would have been able to depart without regret—

because it was a decision she had made herself. What truly matters is having resolve when despair strikes.

The Buddha has this to say, in my loosely reinterpreted version:

> When you're at your lowest, you need to calm down. You need to take a good look at yourself and find the best way forward. That's the only way. It's the fool's way to panic, get lost and lose sight of yourself. Even if you're going to die, is there any need to get even darker? Since you're going to die anyway, why not try to be as cheerful as you can until then?

There is hope that can only be born from despair. Never forget that.

How to Break Through the Wall of Wanting

What is the difference between admiration and envy? Many of us as children were frequently asked, "What do you want to be when you grow up?" Back then, with pure hearts, we might have answered, "A professional baseball player!" or "A pop star!"—imagining our future selves with excitement, and with admiration for those who inspired us.

This kind of admiration is similar to envy, but you need to be aware of the slightly different nuance. While admiration involves a vision of an ideal and a heartfelt desire to become like someone, envy is rooted in comparison with others and a sense of resentment or longing.

> *"It must be nice to earn so much money."*
>
> *"It must be nice to live in a big house."*
>
> *"It must be nice to drive a luxury car."*
>
> *"It must be nice to be cute and have a great figure."*

These feelings stem from comparing yourself to others and are dependent on external factors, rather than on a personal vision of who you want to become. This is what makes it fundamentally different from the innocent admiration of a child dreaming about their future.

This kind of envy is what Buddhism calls "pride." It is an insatiable desire, born from our inability to stop measuring ourselves against those around us. In Buddhist teachings, envy is considered one of the "worldly desires" that should be discarded.

There is no end to comparing yourself to others. More money, a bigger house, a fancier car, better looks . . .

This "more, more, more" mentality is an endless cycle—envy will never be satisfied, no matter how much you gain.

But this is not the case with admiration. You have an ideal image that you envision for yourself, and you are the driving force behind your own efforts to achieve it. This is a beautiful and meaningful mindset—a force that fuels self-improvement and growth.

If you are consumed by envy and constantly comparing yourself to others, you will never find true happiness. Instead of pursuing your own dreams, you will spend your life chasing after others, driven by feelings of inferiority or superiority. This can lead to a bitter and unsatisfying existence—one where you never truly feel at peace with yourself. Living with envy means never being content, always craving more and ultimately wasting your life in dissatisfaction.

Has Your Admiration Turned to Envy?

If there is one thing I would like to emphasize it is this: don't envy, but admire. Admiration something that can drive people to grow. It is something that can be used as fuel for self-improvement.

Envy arises when we see someone we feel is doing better than us, but it is never directed at those we perceive as inferior. Let's say you find yourself asking: "Why is this person so good at what they do?"

You should not compare yourself with that person, but rather observe them carefully and strive to be like them.

But when this mindset goes in the wrong direction—when it turns negative—it becomes bitterness and resentment:

"Why do they get all the luck?"

"Someone like me could never . . ."

Before you know it, those thoughts will mutate into:

"They really get on my nerves."

"I want to see them fail."

This is where envy becomes toxic jealousy, which poisons the heart. Through my YouTube channel, *Osho Taigu's One Question & One Answer*, I have heard countless people share their struggles, and time and time again, I see this pattern—envy, left unchecked, leads to suffering. But admiration leads to growth and fulfillment.

Can you put in the same effort as that person you envy?

Ignorance Gives Rise to Jealousy

Some people are clearly sarcastic toward me, and I can't help but wonder why. Perhaps they think that because I'm a Buddhist monk I won't argue back.

At the temple, I often encounter people who say things that seem deliberately unkind. For example, we've recently been upgrading our buildings to make them more comfortable for visitors, such as improving the bathroom facilities and adding air-conditioning and heating to the main hall. So I get comments like "I see COVID-19 didn't stop the temple from making money then," or "Buddhist monks are really making a killing, aren't they?"

When I was ignorant and lacking in training, I would get upset over such remarks or feel hurt inside, thinking, "That's not how it is at all.

But now I respond in a different way. "If you are so envious of our lifestyle, why don't you become a monk yourself? Do you want to get up at four o'clock in the morning, 365 days a year for five or ten years? No matter how cold or snowy it gets, we have to clean the temple barefoot. Would you like to join us?"

Strangely enough, every time I say this, they immediately reply, "Oh no, that's quite alright!"

I'm not trying to claim that monks alone bear unique hardships, but if someone truly feels envious of my life, I believe the best way for them to understand it is to experience it firsthand.

I also believe that if they actually became a monk, they would see for themselves that they would not make a whole lot of money.

In the end, ignorance leads to suffering. If we knew the reality of a particular situation from the beginning, we would surely not be envious.

Anyone who appears to have something worth envying has undoubtedly put in unseen effort and endured hardships. Many celebrities with great figures may go to the gym five times a week for rigorous workouts, or they may resist their favorite foods and pay attention to their diet in order to stay in shape.

Perhaps you're thinking, "Well, those people must have been blessed with good qualities to begin with," but it takes a certain amount of effort to maintain something, no matter what it is.

When I was a child, I used to think that I wanted to be an astronaut, and I dreamed of traveling to outer space. But when I learned about the harsh reality of this profession—the years of intense training to be undertaken, the grueling physical and mental endurance required and the dangers of spending months confined in a spacecraft with your life constantly at risk—I realized there was no way I could handle that, and so I ended up giving up on the dream without a second thought.

When I mentioned earlier that I suggest to those who think monks have it easy to give our lifestyle a try, I am not trying to be provocative when I say this. I simply want to emphasize that if you are jealous of someone's job, whether it's a highly specialized profession or a more ordinary role, actually trying it yourself—or even just imagining what it would be like—completely changes your perspective. When you do that, careless envy naturally disappears.

Where Is Your Dissatisfaction Really Directed?

Many people spend their days feeling dissatisfied.

> *"I just can't accept this situation."*

> *"I always feel that something is missing in my life."*

There may be various reasons for this kind of dissatisfaction—perhaps you feel your abilities are lacking, or your environment isn't ideal. Whatever the cause, living with a constant sense of unease and frustration can be exhausting. Dissatisfaction is an emotion that arises when your desires are not being fulfilled, whether caused by internal or external factors.

> **The first thing to consider when you feel dissatisfied is "Who is the object of my dissatisfaction?"**

Are you dissatisfied with yourself? Or are you dissatisfied with someone else? Understanding this distinction is key to figuring out how to manage and address these feelings.

First, let's look at dissatisfaction with yourself:

> *"I'm still only getting paid this much."*

> *"I really want to do a different job."*

> *"There are so many things I want to do, but I don't have enough time."*

The above types of dissatisfaction stem from not being satisfied with your current state, and it comes from within.

This kind of dissatisfaction with yourself is not necessarily a bad thing.

> **Dissatisfaction can be an emotion that provides motivation and ambition, and can also serve as a source of growth and development in the future.**

Dissatisfaction with others, however, serves little purpose.

"That person's behavior drives me crazy."

"I get frustrated when my staff don't do what I want them to do."

"The company refuses to raise my salary."

This type of dissatisfaction—directed at people other than yourself, such as friends, family or colleagues—brings no benefit at all.

> **Frustration with others does not help you grow; it is a useless emotion that only leads to stress.**

Behind these feelings lie the hidden thoughts:

"I want more of this."

"Why can't you do that for me?"

At its core, this dissatisfaction stems from the belief that "I" should be treated with the highest priority." When that expectation isn't met, frustration builds, fueling feelings of resentment that can turn into anger:

"Why am I the only one going through this?"

Does Your Food Taste Good?

As I mentioned earlier, holding on to dissatisfaction toward others will only cause you stress. Also, if the other person does not even know that you are dissatisfied, you are just agonizing in your own mind, and it is completely irrelevant to them.

"My boss is useless—this office is unbelievable!"

"My partner won't do any chores or childcare."

"So-and-so is always bragging—it's so annoying."

People who constantly complain about others are, in a way, like someone who keeps eating food they know tastes bad. If you really want to do something about your current situation, the best way to change it is to clearly communicate your dissatisfaction to the other person and try to work toward a solution. Another option is to throw away or separate yourself from the food that tastes bad.

Also, as I am sure many of you have realized, it is very difficult to change others. There is nothing wrong with telling a useless boss, an unreliable partner or an unpleasant friend how you honestly feel, but it is unlikely that it will dramatically improve their attitude toward you. Each person has their own ego and beliefs. So even if you want them to do things a certain way, they have their own ideas of how things should be. Spending your precious time and emotional energy on something unlikely to change is a huge waste.

If your dissatisfaction is just a light complaint, talking about it can help release stress and even build solidarity with others.

To avoid exhausting yourself over things that cannot be changed, it's important to recognize when to step away, let go or accept the situation with a different mindset.

Believing You Are Right Fuels Suffering

Some people are easily dissatisfied with others and their surroundings, while others are not so easily dissatisfied. Where does this difference come from?

Feelings of dissatisfaction can be related to a strong sense of "ego," as discussed in Chapter 1. In modern terms, this could be described as "ego-driven." Such individuals tend to think, "It's not my fault! It's their fault!"—always believing that they are right. They struggle to accept a reality where the most important person in the world—"me"—is suffering a disadvantage. This kind of suffering comes from an inability to accept that reality.

"From my perspective, you are way out of line."

People who fall into this way of thinking have an excessive attachment to their own desires, which means they are poisoned by an insatiable craving that can never be satisfied. Since they firmly believe they are never at fault, they feel like they are always the victim. And even if they declare, "It's all X's fault!"—in many cases, this is simply shifting responsibility onto others.

In Buddhism, there is a teaching that emphasizes the importance of "knowing enough." This phrase means to be aware of your own limits and not to ask for more than is necessary.

> **Since dissatisfaction is an emotion that stimulates our basic sense of "self," the heart of a person who is constantly dissatisfied with others and his surroundings will remain in a perpetual state of suffering.**

It may be a matter of how someone perceives a particular situation, but it could be said that dissatisfaction keeps growing precisely because a person is convinced that they are never at fault.

Consider these two statements:

> *"I'm still only getting paid this much."*

> *"The company is not raising my salary at all."*

They may seem similar, but actually they are quite different. In response to dissatisfaction about a low salary, the first perspective could be that of a person wondering if their own abilities might be lacking. Meanwhile, the second perspective does not even consider for a moment that their own abilities could be the issue. That kind of thinking is a misunderstanding—or more accurately, a sign of ignorance.

If someone is highly skilled, working hard, and yet finds

themselves deliberately being underpaid by an exploitative company, that's a different story. But the first step should be to objectively assess yourself and ask, "Am I truly performing at a level that matches my salary?" Self-reflection is crucial.

We often hear stories of people losing their jobs because of poor company performance. Many may feel intense dissatisfaction or anger toward their employer as a result.

So who was truly at a disadvantage in this situation—the employee who was let go, or the company that let them go? If you were truly needed by the company, you might not have lost your job. I realize this may sound harsh, but maybe—just maybe—you hadn't realized that your evaluation of yourself was completely different to the company's evaluation of you.

You Can't Control the Hearts of Others

Dissatisfaction with others—or in other words, unfulfilled desires—stems from being trapped in a state of "greed," bound by the belief that "things should be this way." When things do not go as you wish, that frustration can turn into anger.

As mentioned earlier, the gap between how you see yourself and how others see you creates unfulfilled desires. To bridge this gap, it is not enough to focus on what you think of yourself.

> **You must understand how others perceive you. Failing to recognize this—due to ignorance—can lead to unfortunate outcomes for yourself.**

If you really want to solve the problem of dissatisfaction, you have be sure of where your dissatisfaction lies. If you are

Don't waste your energy on things beyond your control.

dissatisfied with yourself, use it as an incentive to improve and aim higher. If your dissatisfaction is directed at other people, however, recognize that it originates from your own ego. In such cases, it is best to let go—either by distancing yourself from the situation, accepting it for what it is or making peace with it. You can work on yourself, but you can't work on others, so worrying about what to do about someone else is pointless. Complaining about things that are out of your control is a waste of energy. Instead, shift your mindset—recognize this as unnecessary effort, and guide yourself toward a lighter, more peaceful heart.

We Cannot Force Our Self-esteem to Rise

The same words can either bring comfort or cause stress, depending on how they are received. For example, the term "self-esteem" is generally seen in a positive light. Recently, there has been a trend encouraging people to "boost their self-esteem," implying that those with low self-esteem find life a struggle. Bookstores are filled with guides on raising self-esteem, and countless seminars are held on the topic. According to psychological research, there are two types of self-esteem, implicit and explicit:

- **Implicit self-esteem:** an unconscious sense of self-worth
- **Explicit self-esteem:** the self-worth you are consciously aware of

Even though we often refer to "self-esteem" as a single concept, the two types of self-esteem above differ significantly.

From a Buddhist perspective, individuals with both high implicit and explicit self-esteem tend to have a stable mind.

But those with low implicit self-esteem who try to forcibly raise their explicit self-esteem often become arrogant and develop narcissistic tendencies. These individuals may conspicuously act as if they have high self-esteem. When faced with situations that threaten their self-image—such as criticism or a decline in status—they desperately attempt to maintain their self-worth through self-hypnosis-like positive thinking: "I'm amazing!" "I'm so much better than that person!"

In short, because these individuals have an extreme fear of losing their self-esteem, they consciously try to raise their outward self-esteem, forcing themselves to maintain it—often through great effort. This could be considered a rather unhealthy behavior—almost pathological—because it leads to excessive self-defense mechanisms, which in turn makes it easier for mental and physical health to deteriorate. There is nothing wrong with wanting to improve self-esteem or making an effort to do so. But there is a saying that "90 percent of human behavior is unconscious," meaning that the core of a person cannot be easily changed. In other words, no matter how much someone outwardly proclaims, "I am amazing!" or "I love myself!"—if their implicit self-esteem remains low and they lack true confidence, eventually the cracks will begin to show.

The Burden of Vanity

Vanity—the desire to present yourself in a better light—can be extremely troublesome. For example, there are many celebrities who, despite appearing bright, positive and full of energy on the surface, end up struggling with mental health issues, turning to drugs or, in the worst cases, taking their own lives. These kinds of stories are not uncommon. Most likely, the persona they present through television and media is vastly different from their true self. This highlights a crucial point: explicit self-esteem alone is not enough. We often see famous people who, after a scandal, make a show of reflecting on their actions and attempt to redeem themselves through new achievements, as they strive to make a comeback. But as far as I'm concerned, if changing your heart were that simple, nobody would struggle.

"Let me do some zazen to repent!"

"I made a mistake, let me train with Priest Taigu!"

There are many entertainers, athletes and company executives who come to Fukugonji Temple with such requests but I have consistently refused to accept them.

I'm not saying this applies to all of them, but the majority are simply looking to showcase their Buddhist experience in order to capture it on camera to regain public trust. Some even bring a professional photographer with them. This is exactly why the saying "actions speak louder than words" holds true. No matter how much superficial training certain people undergo, their character does not change. If someone is truly committed to reflecting on their actions, they should do so quietly. The moment they broadcast what they are doing on television or on social media, their intent is no longer about genuine self-improvement—it's driven by the desire to look good.

There many people who appear humble but in reality are deeply vain.

Be Aware of What You Can and Cannot Do

People who truly have confidence in themselves—on a deep, subconscious level—do not become vain in the first place. This idea is not just found in Buddhism, it is also recognized in psychology. Those who carry some internal instability—such as personal insecurities or complexes—often work humbly to overcome them. But there is one very important point that I want everyone to remember:

> **Self-esteem cannot be raised simply by deciding to raise it.**

Affirmations (the practice of making positive declarations to become your ideal self) may have temporary effects, but in the end, they rely on comparison with others—which is a form of pride. As long as someone is constantly measuring themselves against others, they will never find true peace.

> **True mental stability comes from remaining unfazed, whether you are praised or criticized.**

If you find yourself forcing positive thinking, it is proof that your heart is already unsettled.

Once you realize that vanity is a form of pride and stop wasting energy on comparisons with others, humility will naturally follow. Humility does not mean self-deprecation, such as saying, "Oh no, I'm nothing special . . ." True humility is about clearly understanding what you can do and what

Forcing yourself to think positively can have the opposite effect.

you cannot do. It means being able to see yourself objectively.

Those who are considered "top-tier" in their fields understand their own limitations. That is precisely why they are never satisfied with themselves. You won't hear a truly great person boldly proclaim, "I'm amazing!" It is their relentless pursuit of growth that makes them professionals. People who can objectively assess both their strengths and weaknesses with a level head will continue to improve. The moment you become vain, you have already fallen to mediocrity. This is something worth engraving in your heart.

Looking Down on Others Does Not Elevate You

I explained "pride" in detail on page 126. It is the impulse to judge others as superior, inferior or equal to you. The negative emotion that arises from this pride is "contempt." It emerges when we see another as beneath us and we look down on them or mock them. This is not an innate human instinct, but rather a deeply "social emotion."

Contempt is an emotion that we do not need in our lives. It is meaningless and worthless and should be dismissed.

Suppose you despise someone:

"He's less educated than me, so he's not worth much."

"Look at all the makeup she's wearing to try and make herself look pretty."

A sense of petty superiority, such as thinking "I'm better than that other person," is a distraction from happiness.

Thinking this way may give you a fleeting sense of superiority. But nothing actually changes.

Even if your contempt is based on objective facts, it does not improve your abilities or make you more attractive.

The same is true for celebrity scandals. Some people, feeling they could never compete with an idol or actor in terms of looks, wealth or fame, seize the opportunity to attack them when they are caught in a scandal or romantic affair:

"I never thought they were the kind of person who'd do that."

"At least I don't cheat. At least I don't use drugs."

Saying things like this implies you are right, they are wrong and you're a better person than they are. But what is the point of that? No amount of antagonism on your part will cause any change in yourself or your surroundings. And even if you genuinely wanted the celebrity to reflect on what they have done, since you have no actual connection to them there is no way that your words would reach their hearts or make them decide to behave differently.

This kind of antagonism is behind the problem of trolling, where people post negative comments about others online, pushing a person into a corner and possibly contributing to a tragic outcome.

Contempt brings no discipline, no redemption.

Moreover, harboring irritation and contempt will have a negative impact on your body and mind, making you the one who suffers in the end. This is something I hope you will recognize first and foremost.

Be There for Others

If you find yourself feeling contempt for someone, first calmly analyze the type of contempt that you are feeling. If your feelings are more akin to pity, such as "too bad," or " poor you," then try to shift your perspective from contempt to sympathy. Sympathy is not a definitive solution to a problem, but it is far better than contempt. Sympathy allows you to understand the other person's emotions and to offer compassion to that person.

> **Failing to consider the underlying reasons behind someone's actions or their true intentions is considered an act of ignorance in Buddhism.**

For example, let's say someone has extremely poor table manners or uses rough language. You may find yourself reacting with contempt:

> *"This is terrible!"*
>
> *"What a hopeless person!"*
>
> *"I never want to be like that."*

Instead, perhaps you could try considering:

"Maybe they didn't grow up in a good environment."

"Perhaps their upbringing lacked proper guidance and it's not entirely their fault."

"Maybe they're having a hard time emotionally."

The Buddha's view is that all human beings are equally ignorant, and that everyone carries some form of illness. There is no such thing as a perfect person. Instead of wasting our time looking down on other people, we should offer them our compassion.

"That's just the way they are."

"It's not entirely their fault."

If you can think this way, you won't allow negative emotions to take root in your heart. Your state of mind will surely become more peaceful than it is now.

Much of Contempt Develops into Anger

Contempt often includes emotions that are closer to anger rather than mere disdain.

"Why can't that person do something as simple as this? Unbelievable."

"This is such a narrow street, and they're walking spread out side by side—how inconsiderate and annoying."

The contempt that arises toward those who cannot do what you can easily do, who cannot read the room or who cannot follow social rules, usually develops into anger.

When it comes to celebrity scandals, people may lash out in anger, saying things like: "I thought they were pure and innocent, but they broke the rules and had an affair. That's unforgivable!"

If you realize that your feeling of looking down on someone has turned into anger, please take the measures to deal with anger described on page 59—such as not fueling the fire of anger with unnecessary speculation, or distancing yourself from the source of anger. If you fail to notice that your contempt has turned to anger, you may become even more angry and create troublesome situations for yourself.

One common reaction, particularly among Japanese people, is making sarcastic remarks that are just loud enough for the other person to hear.

"Oh dear, this is a public place."

"It takes some nerve to do something like that."

Since these remarks stem from a feeling of contempt, they inevitably carry a certain unpleasant tone. Naturally, the person on the receiving end will feel offended. Even if they acknowledge their own wrongdoing, they may become angry at the person who made the snide comment. It wouldn't be surprising if such exchanges escalate into arguments.

If you feel contempt for someone who does not follow social rules and that contempt is about to turn into anger, it would be much better for both parties if you take a deep breath and calmly point out the problem to them.

If a person is confronted with a logical and well-reasoned argument, delivered politely and without a sarcastic or confrontational tone, they are more likely to accept it and comply.

However, if the person is a stranger and you don't want to risk a possible escalation of the problem into a violent argument, it's best to separate yourself from the anger-inducing situation.

What I Learned from a Non-sarcastic Foreigner

I had an experience during my student years that left a strong impression on me.

One day, I boarded a crowded train with a lot of luggage, including a large bag containing my karate uniform and protective gear, and placed the luggage at my feet. Naturally, the other passengers looked at me disapprovingly, as if to say, "You are in the way."

I was aware of this, but since I had so much baggage I didn't think there was much I could do.

Then, a foreign man who boarded the train after me said, "Your luggage is in the way, so please put it on the rack."

I was surprised that he suddenly spoke to me, and for a moment I was alarmed. But there was nothing angry or sarcastic about him at all. He simply seemed to be telling me that he thought it would be better for both of us if I did as he suggested. Then he helped me put the heavy bags on the luggage rack.

If someone had said to me, "You are in the way," or "You are being thoughtless," my younger self would have been irritated at the time.

But to the man who nonchalantly pointed out my error and helped me, I was filled with gratitude. This experience made me realize that even when people have the same feelings about a situation, the way in which they communicate those feelings makes a huge difference in how the message is received. The Japanese tend to be relatively shy and not very good at making such points to others or saying things clearly. Perhaps we can learn from people like this foreigner, who addressed the problem straightforwardly and without unnecessary disapproval.

How to Change Your Mental Habits

In Chapter 1, I explained the basic concepts of Buddhism when viewed as psychology, as well as the mechanisms through which various worries and suffering arise. And in chapters 2 to 4, I introduced the characteristics of typical negative emotions and how to let go of them, dividing them into three categories: greed, anger and ignorance.

If you understand, learn and put into practice the information I have conveyed to you, you will be able to live a happier life, with a more peaceful mind and less stress and worries about your relationships with others.

In this chapter, I will give you some information to help you make more effective use of what we have discussed so far. I will share some tips to help you understand your own heart more deeply and let go of your worries and suffering more skillfully. The first topic is the Buddhist way of understanding the heart and the fundamental stance toward it.

How to Cultivate a Good Heart

After thoroughly considering the question,"What is the heart?" the Buddha's conclusion was:

> **The heart is like a vessel filled with liquid, where all kinds of emotional elements are dissolved.**

Make it a habit to fill
your heart with
good things.

And he gave these emotional elements the name "mental factors."

Just as tea is made by steeping tea leaves in water and coffee is made by passing ground coffee beans through a coffee grinder, the contents of the heart change depending on what you dissolve it in.

There are various types of mental factors, but they can be categorized into three groups:

- **25 positive mental factors**
- **14 negative mental factors**
- **13 neutral mental factors**

Letting go of the negative mental factors of anger, envy and contempt, and cultivating the positive mental factors of joy, affection and compassion—this is the eternal theme of Buddhism.

Whether someone is regarded as a good person or a villain, both positive and negative mental factors exist that person. However, the strength and dominance of these factors will differ depending on a person's innate personality, upbringing and circumstances. Someone widely regarded as unpleasant, or a bad person likely has a mind where negative mental factors have become dominant. You can become aware of whether negative mental factors have become dominant in your own mind by calmly reflecting on yourself. Then, by consciously suppressing or eliminating negative mental factors and striving to strengthen positive ones, you can shift the balance toward a more positive mind.

Forming Positive Habits

Those devoted to the Buddhist path engage in practice to let go of negative mental factors and cultivate positive mental factors, but the practice referred to here is not about enduring hardships, pushing through difficulties or striving to achieve something through sheer effort.

> **Buddhist practice is about developing habits that naturally allow positive mental factors to remain dominant. It is about reaching a state where good thoughts arise effortlessly, good behavior comes naturally and good words flow spontaneously.**

In other words, it is about forming unconscious habits.

Buddhism often involves group practice, which creates a mutually beneficial effect. The purpose is for practitioners to be in an environment where they are aware of each other, refine their practice together, and mutually elevate one another. It's like being in an elite sports team. The team becomes strong because it has talented players, a skilled coach and other excellent staff, and they practice at a high level.

Among the negative mental factors mentioned on the previous page, there are some that act as poisons that corrode the heart. Some are so potent that they can be described as deadly toxins, possessing an intensely negative power. Before these things take control of your heart, try to discard them as much as possible, and even if you can't get rid of them completely, try to reduce their influence on you every day. At the same time, work on expanding and strengthening the positive mental factors.

As you do so, your heart will become brighter, broader, stronger and more compassionate. Even if it's just little by little, aim to purify the liquid in your heart.

While this book primarily focuses on negative mental factors, which were discussed in detail in chapters 2 to 4, a summary of each of the positive and neutral mental factors is provided at the end of the book. I hope you will find it helpful.

Now, let's talk about the Buddhist philosophy of existence—specifically, how the things and events we see and feel exist, where and in what way they exist, and how humans perceive them.

In Buddhism, it is believed that humans can perceive existence through six sensory faculties:

- **eyes (sight)**
- **ears (hearing)**
- **nose (smell)**
- **tongue (taste)**
- **body (touch)**
- **mind (consciousness)**

The first five correspond to our standard five senses. These allow us to perceive things that exist in front of us as real, tangible entities.

The sixth sense, refers to the mind itself. It is unique in that it allows us to recognize things that are not physically present, such as past memories or future possibilities.

And this sometimes causes problems.

We regret the past. We imagine a negative future. These thoughts can become the seeds of suffering. For example, you had a quarrel with your partner last night, and you're still angry about it this morning. Or perhaps a hurtful remark from a friend lingers in your mind for years, resurfacing again and again, making you think, "I'll never forgive them," fueling your anger and sadness. But these emotions—this anger and sorrow—are not caused by something that physically exists in front of you right now. They are creations of your own mind—mere illusions.

Your heart is consciously reacting to something that is no longer present, inviting anger and sadness upon itself.

All Existence is within You

Now, let's consider the question: where does existence truly reside? This includes not only things that seem real and tangible in front of you but also the very nature of their existence. This idea might sound a bit abstract, so let's break it down simply:

- **Is the existence of "things and events" outside of you or inside of you?**

Decide to live with the mindset that most things are a delusion.

- **How do you perceive their existence?**

For example, imagine there is a bicycle placed in front of you. Would you say this bicycle exists outside of you or inside of you? When asked this question, almost everyone would probably answer "outside." But the bicycle actually exists within you. The bicycle, which is projected onto the brain through the lens of the eye, only exists when our mind perceives that the bicycle exists there. When you explain to someone that "there is a bicycle here," the "here" you are referring to is the place that is recognized in your mind. Therefore, in Buddhism, it is thought to be inside, not outside.

In short, Buddhism is the idea that everything that exists in this world is within ourselves.

Furthermore, all things are subject to impermanence—they are constantly changing. Nothing remains eternal. Even when considering "the self," you have to ask: "Which version of me, at what moment in time, under what circumstances?" In other words, there is no such thing as a fixed, unchanging self. What's more, we tend to add unnecessary fantasies to the things and events inside us, making them bigger or changing them in some way. So, what you perceive as "reality" may actually be nothing more than an illusion—a hollow construct, far removed from its true nature.

Before you can face any suffering you are going through, you first need to understand the mechanisms of the mind. It is natural and inevitable for suffering to arise in the mind. Bear in mind though that most of it is nothing more than an illusion, mixed with delusions that you have created yourself—meaning that you have the power to change it.

Try to think about it this way:

> *"I am just freely creating illusions in my own mind and then reacting to them on my own"*

If you understand this, you can soften the shock you feel when something difficult happens, even if you can't stop yourself from feeling negative emotions. What would have felt like an earthquake of magnitude 10 in your emotional world could instead be reduced to a 2 or 3. By consciously training your mind to accept this perspective, you will gradually stop being shaken by every negative emotion that arises.

I have already emphasized the importance of focusing on your inner mind and clearly recognizing what is happening within you.

> **This continued awareness through focused attention is what is referred to in Buddhism as "meditation."**

The Buddha devoted his life to observing the process by which suffering is created in the mind. Meditation is the process of becoming aware of what Buddhism classes as the Three Poisons—greed, anger and ignorance—within yourself. If you do not face your own mind, you will not be able to let go of your suffering.

Tips for Cooling Down Your Anger

One of the core emotions that fuels suffering is anger. To calm anger, it is essential to view situations rationally and objectively. The method involves four steps:

Meditation is the practice of noticing the shifts in your own mind.

1. Focus on your mind

2. Observe it

3. Recognize it

4. Transcend it

This is my approach to meditation.

For example, let's say you're really angry with someone who has done something you can't forgive. How can you deal with such a situation rationally? I advise people that when they feel overwhelmed by anger they should write down the reasons why they are angry. Then they should ask themselves what it is they want from the other person.

When people actually try this method, many of them end up realizing that what they were angry about wasn't such a big deal after all. If I ask them to show what they've written down to someone else, some of them become embarrassed. The key here is the act of calmly observing your own emotions and taking time to reflect—that process itself is what truly matters.

When your emotions start to run wild, you can lose sight of yourself, but by reflecting on and analyzing the situation, you can regain clarity. Thinking about the situation in a logical way and calmly identifying the facts behind your emotions—through writing down the reason for your anger and asking yourself what you want from the other person—will help your feelings of anger naturally subside. In other words:

Emotions are like an accelerator, and rationality is like a brake.

You don't have to sit in zazen to meditate.

If you continue to let yourself be overtaken by anger, this will become like an infection of your mind and body, ultimately causing more harm to you than anyone else.

Once you've mastered the art of letting go of anger by writing things down, let's try practicing the final step of the four-step meditation process, "Transcend it."

For example, if there is someone at work who you absolutely cannot stand, you could improve your performance to the extent that you stand out in your area of expertise, and eventually rise to a position of leadership over them. That's the idea.

Turning anger into motivation doesn't always work out positively, but it's more effective than just moping around, and if you succeed, you can solve your problems and improve your own skills at the same time, so it's a win-win situation.

I once heard a story about a figure skater who had won a gold medal at the Olympics, and how she had worked hard to overcome her difficult experiences. She was an athlete who had attracted a lot of attention since she was a child, and she had sometimes felt frustrated when the media wrote terrible articles about her that were completely untrue. So, what did she do? Instead of being consumed by resentment, she studied the media industry in depth, learned how it operated and even made an effort to understand the perspective of the journalists who interviewed her.

If you can use the negative emotions you feel to improve your abilities, you've hit the jackpot. The saying "A crisis is an opportunity" holds true—whether you harness your frustration or let it defeat you is entirely up to you.

Distinguishing between Reality and Delusion

In your heart, suffering is often created not only from your own experiences but also from influences and conditioning from parents and those around you. These preconceived ideas shape your emotions and perceptions, sometimes leading to delusional suffering that is not based on reality.

> **Meditation is the process of sorting through the information you've absorbed and clearly distinguishing between facts and delusions. Through this, you begin to recognize what emotions you are truly experiencing.**

For example, imagine you are angry because your romantic partner hasn't bothered to contact you in a while. At first you think you are angry, but when you take time to face your emotions honestly, you may realize that beneath the anger, there is a feeling of sadness or loneliness—a desire to be cared for more.

Emotions come and go, and as things continue to move without pause, your own perceptions will also change at a dizzying pace.

We are creatures who experience the intensity of being alive not only through our senses, but also when something touches our hearts.

Whether they are good or bad feelings, it is important to continue to be aware of the changes in your own heart while facing both types of feelings squarely.

The key elements of meditation are concentration, observation and awareness. Ultimately, the goal is to be able to control your own mind, but first of all, it is important to be able to see things from a correct perspective—called "right view" in Buddhism—rather than from your own personal point of view.

Right view means to see existence and phenomena as they are. We tend to twist reality through the lens of our personal assumptions, biases and emotions, making it difficult to perceive things as they truly are.

Each of us sees the world through our own personal filter, and naturally there will be different perceptions. Yet, people often believe that their own perspective is the correct, objective truth, failing to recognize that their view is merely subjective.

If we fail to acknowledge this discrepancy, we struggle to understand differing opinions, which leads to conflicts and misunderstandings.

In order to avoid this, we need wisdom—the ability to discern truth. The only way to open up this wisdom is through meditation. At the same time, traditional Buddhist teachings emphasize that in addition to the technique of meditation itself, it is also important to create an environment conducive to meditation. To truly focus on your inner self and deeply reflect, you must avoid environments where excessive stimuli constantly invade your senses.

Think about when you need to work or study—do you ever find yourself mindlessly surfing the Internet or checking social media on your phone? Your mind drifts from one place to another, unable to stay still. If this sounds familiar, then you likely understand the importance of creating a stable environment that minimizes distractions.

What kind of diet, lifestyle and daily routine foster a state conducive to meditation? Buddhism involves reexamining your entire way of life, including clothing, food and shelter, in order to create the best conditions for meditation. If you ever have the chance to take part in a meditation retreat at a Buddhist temple, I highly recommend this as a way of experiencing a structured and supportive environment for inner reflection.

Training the Unconscious Mind for Modern Life

Through our senses, we take in information from the world—and how we interpret that information is the essence of Buddhist practice. There is a fifth-century Buddhist text called *Visuddhimagga* that summarizes the practices of Buddhist monks in ancient India. Let's take a look at one of the training methods from that time.

Today, when a person dies, it is usual to hold a funeral and burial or cremation. In ancient India, however, it was not uncommon for corpses to be left in the mountains. As part of their training, monks would travel to these sites and observe the decaying bodies for long periods of time. This may sound unbelievable, but it was considered a legitimate meditation practice. The purpose was to observe one's own emotional state while witnessing decay—"What thoughts and feelings arise within me as I watch this?" Though this may seem drastically different from what we commonly imagine as meditation, there exist countless techniques for achieving deep concentration—some of which, like this, may even seem extreme or unsettling.

Observing corpses as a form of meditation is, of course, impractical in modern times. But practices that have a similar underlying purpose still exist in our lives today. For example, in baseball, there is a popular fielding drill where players are repeatedly made to run and catch ground balls. This is done not just to improve their defensive skills, but to train their bodies to react instinctively to the bounce of the ball and the timing of throws—allowing them to perform these actions without thinking.

Buddhist training follows the same principle.

By repeatedly making good choices, speaking good words and performing good actions, the goal is to develop a way of life where goodness flows naturally and unconsciously.

In essence, it is no different from sports or cooking, where consistent practice allows the body to move automatically. Buddhism is not about mystical experiences. In fact, the Buddha rejected extreme ascetic practices, such as standing under waterfalls for purification, walking through mountains without food or water for days, or engaging in acts that create the illusion of achieving supernatural strength. While such practices are not necessarily wrong, the Buddha believed that "those actions alone will not lead to enlightenment." I also often emphasize that "meditation is not just about sitting in the lotus position." Simply sitting in meditation posture without real inner focus will not bring any transformation.

Rather than becoming fixated on seated meditation, you should find a method that allows you to truly concentrate on your own mind.

Superficial Imitation Creates a Vicious Circle

Many people may have the image of Buddhist monks as individuals who deliver meaningful and inspiring talks. In Japan, Buddhist monks give sermons at memorial services, and it is not uncommon for monks to be invited to corporate lectures to share insights as well.

I, too, have had opportunities to speak at such events, and through my YouTube channel, *Osho Taigu's One Question & One Answer*, I try and address people's concerns.

This does not mean that I accept every request indiscriminately. For instance, I often receive invitations to teach mindfulness in connection with Buddhist meditation. But these days, I politely decline. The reason is that learning mindfulness as a mere how-to technique carries potential risks if its true essence is misunderstood.

Requests to teach mindfulness often come from companies that want to use meditation as a tool to reduce employee stress. I once visited a company that had made such a request, and what I witnessed was deeply unsettling—the very structure of the company and its working environment were the root causes of employee stress. It almost felt as if they were asking me to make their employees incapable of feeling stress or even to numb their minds. To put it bluntly, this is like an abuser asking a therapist, "Can you make the victim stop feeling the pain of domestic violence?" In such workplaces, the real solution is not mindfulness training. Instead, what is truly needed is fundamental reform—creating a work environment where employees don't accumulate stress in the first place.

Certain notorious cults have gone as far as labeling abuse as "guidance." A charismatic leader might say, "The reason I

If you misunderstand the true nature of mindfulness, it can become a trap.

hit you is because I care about you." Such ways of thinking are extremely dangerous.

In Japan, the concept of "self-responsibility" is often emphasized, and when it comes to mind control, there is a tendency to blame the victim, with statements like "If you were deceived, it's your own fault."

When something becomes fashionable, such as meditation, most people tend to want to just copy the superficial aspects of things, rather than the essence. Just copying the superficial aspects of things will not lead to a fundamental solution. Companies who want mindfulness training may not have bad intentions, but the issue lies in their superficial approach—instead of reevaluating employee work environments and structures, they are simply chasing trends by saying, "Teach us mindfulness because it's popular right now!" while failing to grasp its true essence.

Meditation, at its core, is about focusing and becoming aware of the fundamental nature of things.

If this is not understood and it is merely imitated as a tool, it is inevitable that it will lead in the wrong direction.

In this book, I have been talking about how emotions are born in the heart and felt in the heart. This is not incorrect, but there is actually another source that gives rise to emotions besides the heart. That source is the body.

The state of our bodies changes depending on how we perceive and accept things.

Consider for a moment that when something moves us emotionally, we might say "I'm touched." This is a phrase that relates to the physical sensation of something coming into contact with our hearts. Other connections between our physical and emotional states include getting irritable when you are hungry, or being unable to sleep and feeling anxious.

Through dedicated practice, you can learn to recognize emotional shifts through bodily sensations.

In addition to my Buddhist training, I have also trained in karate and worked as a physiotherapist, which has given me a deep, firsthand understanding of how emotional changes manifest physically. Many monks tend to focus solely on the mind, emphasizing the mental and spiritual over the physical. As a result, most Buddhist teachings do not touch much upon the body. My approach is different. I have often said: "Buddhism is easier to explain with your body than with words."

Once a month, I hold events across Japan (and in some international locations), where participants can experience Buddhist teachings through physical awareness. This approach focuses on the body as a gateway to understanding Buddhism, and it has been very well received.

Beings without a physical body do not possess emotions. This is clear evidence that the body and emotions are deeply interconnected.

Learning with Your Body and with Words

The ideal way to learn is through both words and physical experience at the same time. This bodily awareness can only

Making emotions "visible"
is the key to
a peaceful heart.

be developed through accumulated experience, and it is not something that can be fully grasped by words alone. For this reason, I have chosen to touch on the topic briefly here at the end of the book.

To illustrate the feeling of bodily awareness with a relatable example, think of a professional baseball player hitting a home run. When the ball strikes the sweet spot of the bat and soars through the air, this sensation is something that only those who have actually hit a home run at pro level can truly understand. Even if a former pro player with exceptional coaching skills explains it in great detail, an amateur like us would still struggle to grasp the true feeling. Even young baseball players and high school athletes may find it difficult to fully attain the same level of "bodily awareness" that professionals experience.

Buddhism has a similar aspect, which is why I strongly encourage people to not only learn through words but also engage in physical practice.

When you experience what you have learned in words through physical sensation, your understanding deepens even further.

By becoming aware of the movements of the mind and body and successfully "visualizing" your emotions, you can maintain a sense of inner calm and enhance your ability to control your emotions. This is an essential element in mastering the mind, so for those interested, I highly recommend visiting temples that offer physical training experiences in addition to more traditional types of practice.

25 Positive Mental Factors and 13 Neutral Mental Factors in Buddhism

According to Anuruddha, one of the Buddha's ten great disciples, there are a total of fifty-two mental factors that are taught in Buddhism. There are fourteen negative mental factors, and the central focus of this book has been how to overcome them. In addition to these, there are twenty-five positive mental factors and thirteen fundamental or neutral mental factors that form the foundation of the mind. In this appendix, I will briefly introduce them.

THE 25 POSITIVE MENTAL FACTORS

1. Faith

Faith can be described as a sense of certainty that arises when making correct judgments based on reason and experience. Faith comes from understanding and accepting something through your own reasoning rather than blindly believing in the words of others. Blind faith is considered ignorance and leads to harmful actions.

2. Mindfulness

Mindfulness is the ability to be fully present, noticing what is happening here and now instead of being lost in thoughts of the past or the future. Most of our actions, words and emotions operate on autopilot, influenced by habit. By becoming aware of undesirable actions, speech or thoughts, we can reduce mistakes and conflicts.

3. Shame

Shame is the ability to feel embarrassed about inappropriate or bad behavior. It encompasses the intention to avoid behaving in such a way.

4. Fear of Wrongdoing

This refers to an awareness of the consequences of negative actions and the determination to avoid creating harmful situations. This, together with shame, helps regulate our behavior and prevents wrongdoing. Because these two factors function as a set, they are sometimes referred to collectively as "moral restraint."

5. Lack of Greed

If we lack greed, we have the ability to let go of excessive desire for wealth, knowledge, status or pleasure. True contentment comes from sharing and giving without expecting anything in return. The more a person gives, the more flexible, strong and free the mind becomes.

6. Lack of Hatred

Lack of hatred refers to the cultivation of kindness and compassion toward all beings, which leads to a reduction in anger. When we train ourselves to develop this quality, we can remain calm even when treated unfairly. The key to cultivating a lack of hatred is to avoid judging people based on personal preferences and instead focus on maintaining a kind and gentle heart.

7. Equanimity

This is the ability to maintain a calm state of mind, taking an objective and neutral stance. Developing this trait involves letting go of expectations and treating all beings equally.

8. Physical Relaxation

In this state, the body is at ease and free from tension. This should be the body's natural state. This is closely related to mental relaxation.

9. Mental Relaxation

In this state, the mind is calm and at ease, contributing to both physical and emotional well-being.

10. Physical Agility

Unlike physical relaxation, this refers to a state of liveliness and readiness for action.

11. Mental Agility

This is a state of feeling lighthearted, lively and joyful.

12. Physical Flexibility

The absence of stiffness or pain in the body will contribute to better performance. Growth requires both strength and adaptability. In order to grow, you need to be as supple as a bamboo.

13. Mental Flexibility

Mental flexibility is the opposite of stubbornness. It refers to the ability of the mind to respond to changes in the environment. Water takes the shape of its container, and just as water can adjust to any situation, people who are flexible in their mindset can navigate life more easily and grow continuously.

14. Physical Adaptability

The term physical adaptability refers to a state in which the body functions efficiently and is prepared to take appropriate action at any moment.

15. Mental Adaptability

The psychological state of being ready to take action when needed. Just as a master in martial arts is always prepared for an opponent's attack, this factor refers to the ability to fulfill your role and do what needs to be done. Whether it's work or sports, truly excellent people are not only flexible in body and mind, but also adaptable.

16. Physical Proficiency

This means knowing what you need to do to succeed, and practicing in preparation. Any professional who excels in their field has cultivated both adaptability and physical proficiency.

17. Mental Proficiency

When a person becomes highly trained in a particular field, their mind becomes accustomed to handling all aspects of that field. With continued practice, this mental factor grows. Mental proficiency and physical proficiency develop together.

18. Physical Uprightness

This refers to the ability to persist without giving up and to follow through with actions. It means having inner strength, and consistency in your behavior. When facing a task, instead of hesitating or feeling reluctant, you embrace that task with a sense of initiative.

19. Mental Uprightness
A heart that never gives up. An indomitable spirit. The ability to keep going even after repeated failures. This, along with flexibility, is an essential mental trait for personal growth.

20. Right Speech
The term "right speech" refers to a Buddhist teaching that warns against lying, gossiping, speaking harshly or engaging in meaningless talk. Avoiding harmful speech is known as "right speech." The brain does not distinguish between words spoken to others and words received from others, meaning that harmful speech damages both the speaker and the listener. Therefore, we should always control our speech, and speak mindfully.

21. Right Action
Right action means conducting yourself in a way that does not harm you, others or society. You need to take responsibility for your actions and avoid behaviors that lead to suffering.

22. Right Livelihood
This term refers to the way you earn a living. Even if a job provides financial gain, if it harms you or others, it is best avoided. In the long run, engaging in such work will make it difficult to maintain inner peace. This teaching warns against engaging in work related to killing, stealing, adultery, deceitful speech, weapons trade, alcohol and drug production or trading living beings.

23. Compassion

Compassion is the ability to feel the suffering of others and the motivation to help relieve it. Cultivating compassion brings energy and well-being.

24. Sympathetic Joy

This is the ability to rejoice in the happiness and success of others, for example, feeling happy when a friend gets a promotion, gets married or has a child. While this may seem simple, it can sometimes be difficult because people tend to compare themselves to others and feel jealous.

25. Wisdom

This is the most important of the Buddhist mental factors. It allows you to see things as they truly are, free from personal biases or misconceptions. When wisdom is developed, all other mental factors function correctly. The essence of this teaching is to free yourself from suffering by letting go of attachment and seeing reality clearly.

THE 13 NEUTRAL MENTAL FACTORS

By combining the fundamental mental factors that serve as the foundation of the mind (seven core functions) with the additional mental factors that do not arise in every instance (six supplementary functions), the mechanism by which we perceive and recognize things becomes clearer. This integration of basic and situational mental activities helps us to form a more complete understanding of our experiences.

1. Contact

This refers to the mental function of the mind coming into contact with an object. The six senses in Buddhism—sight, hearing, smell, taste, touch and thought—each interact with their respective objects: the eyes perceive colors and shapes, the ears perceive sounds, the nose perceives scents, the tongue perceives flavors, the body perceives sensations such as heat and texture, and the mind perceives abstract concepts. Through these interactions, the mind itself comes into contact with external objects, leading to recognition.

2. Sensation

This refers to the function of perceiving and experiencing what has been contacted. Even if the senses come into contact with something, recognition does not occur unless there is a corresponding feeling. For example, when the ears perceive a favorite piece of music, it creates a pleasant sensation, while making eye contact with someone you dislike may generate an unpleasant sensation. This demonstrates how our experiences are shaped not only by sensory contact but also by the emotional responses that follow.

3. Recognition

This is the function of distinguishing one object from others. It refers to the impression you form before putting an experience into words. For example, the moment you sees cherry blossoms and autumn leaves and immediately recognize the difference, or the instant you see a round, red fruit hanging from a tree and identifies it as an apple—these are examples of preverbal conceptual recognition.

4. Intention

The term "intention" refers to mental activity that initiates action; a momentary willpower that arises. Human beings express their thoughts through actions, and all actions are determined by their own intentions. Intention is the thought that arises within the mind, such as "I should do this." A weaker form of this is called "inclination," while a stronger form is referred to as "determination."

5. Focused Attention

This is the ability to concentrate on a single object and merge with it. Each of the six senses—sight, hearing, smell, taste, touch and thought—engages in a moment of unity with its respective object when perceiving it. Unlike concentration, which is sustained and deliberate, this is the natural state in which the mind continuously shifts focus to different objects. If nurtured properly, it develops into strong concentration, but if not, the mind becomes scattered.

6. Vitality

This is the continuous arising and ceasing of mental activity. In this system of thought, all things are categorized as either material or mental. The life energy of the physical body is considered one aspect, while the life energy of the mind is another. Living involves a constant cycle of renewal, with cells undergoing change, and metabolism occurring moment by moment. The cessation of this cycle results in death. Similarly, the mind also possesses a transient existence, momentarily coming into being and then fading away. Vitality refers to this instantaneous, ever-renewing activity of the mind.

7. Attention

This is the mental tendency to be drawn toward significant stimuli. The mind naturally gravitates toward striking or engaging objects. Attention is the mechanism that activates the mind. Most people live under the influence of whatever draws their attention rather than exercising conscious control over their own mental states. The Buddha taught, "Live with intention and awareness," and emphasized that gaining control over your own mind leads to true freedom.

8. Initial Application of Thought

This is the ability to process and distinguish information immediately upon encountering an object. It is the logical function that allows us to recognize something instantly, to promote the thought, "What is this?" or "What was that sound?" If something is already clear or does not catch your interest, this function does not activate.

9. Sustained Application of Thought

This function works in tandem with the initial application of thought. While the initial application allows recognition (for example, "What is this? Oh, it's a butterfly."), the sustained application deepens engagement with the object, such as thinking, "I've never seen this type of butterfly before." It is the mental factor that becomes active when you wish to understand something more clearly.

10. Interest

This is the mental factor that causes you to fixate on something, whether in a beneficial or harmful way. Interest can manifest as concentration or as attachment. Examples include: "I must solve this problem," "I can't wait for my new car to be delivered," "Why did that person say that?" or "Where does that person live?" This factor keeps the mind tethered to a specific subject.

11. Effort

The word describes the energy we put into working toward our goals. We can be easily swept away by worldly desires due to the Three Poisons of greed, anger and ignorance, and find it difficult to achieve our goals. But when effort is well-developed, thoughts remain steady and unshaken, making it easier to achieve our objectives. But if effort is focused solely on material pursuits while neglecting mental and emotional refinement, we may fall into a cycle of suffering.

12. Joy

This refers to the happiness and enthusiasm that serve as a source of motivation. Joy manifests in simple pleasures such as savoring a delicious meal, feeling delighted by something or having fun doing something. This feeling drives people to make efforts in life. The joy derived from sensory experiences has its limits, however; when the senses are continuously stimulated, they become desensitized. Something that was once exciting can lose its appeal over time. Instead of constantly seeking external stimulation that costs us time and money, we can cultivate joy by appreciating the small, everyday experiences in life.

13. Desire to Act

This refers to motivation, energy and the ability to take action. When the desire to act weakens, a person may struggle to take action. However, desire to act does not always lead to positive outcomes—it can also manifest in negative ways. Buddhist training helps eliminate the motivation to do bad things and cultivates a strong desire for personal growth and ethical actions. If you cultivate your desire to act, you will become increasingly capable of pursuing meaningful goals.

Afterword

In life there are things that cannot be changed by personal effort, such as natural phenomena; and there are things that can be changed depending on our own actions. For matters beyond our control, we have to accept them. But for things that can be changed through effort, it is better to take action to change them, because doing so makes life much easier. Money, work, relationships and health—all can be improved through effort. And the same applies to your heart.

What kind of image comes to mind when you hear the word "prayer"? Throughout history, when people have faced difficulties, they have turned to prayers to gods and Buddhas. Because of this, many may think of prayer as a plea for divine intervention, asking a deity to grant their wishes.

There are various theories about the origin of this word "prayer," but one of them is that it originates in meaning from "to declare one's intentions." In this sense, prayer means declaring to yourself, "This is what I want to do. This is how I want to be. This is what I will become."

By voicing your intentions through prayer, you can connect with the things you have decided to do, the things you are aiming for, and the things you want to achieve, and work toward them with your own strength, not relying on others. Prayer is not a way of clinging to God or the Buddha, saying "Please grant this for me," or "I wish this would happen," but rather an act of declaring "I will make this happen."

Living with this kind of prayerful mindset is incredibly important. When people experience despair and turn to prayer, even if things do not unfold as they had imagined, they do not feel anger. Because they have declared their own aspirations and done everything they could, there is no regret and no shifting of blame onto others. This resolute way of living is the essence of true prayer. The Buddhist perspective is that prayer is not about weakly pleading with a god to "do something."

The more I continue my own journey of study and practice, the more I think that if more people adopted this way of life, their burdens would feel lighter, and life would become much easier. Of course, reaching such a state requires training and practice, but Buddhism provides a structured and efficient path for this process. Perspectives on Buddhism vary from person to person, and some scholars may disagree with certain interpretations in this book. My goal here has been to share my thoughts and experiences in a way that is as clear and accessible as possible.

Life is painful and difficult.

To live is to constantly experience suffering.

Even so, there are ways to make each day a little brighter, happier and more peaceful. The ideas I have shared in this book are not absolute truths. But if, even for a moment, you thought, "Maybe I should give this a try," or "This might work for me," then I encourage you to give it a go.

From the bottom of my heart, I hope that you can overcome the barriers within your mind, open your heart, let go of even a small portion of your worries and suffering, and walk a life that feels truly fulfilling and happy to you.

—Gensho Taigu

"Books to Span the East and West"

Tuttle Publishing was founded in 1832 in the small New England town of Rutland, Vermont [USA]. Our core values remain as strong today as they were then—to publish best-in-class books which bring people together one page at a time. In 1948, we established a publishing outpost in Japan—and Tuttle is now a leader in publishing English-language books about the arts, languages and cultures of Asia. The world has become a much smaller place today and Asia's economic and cultural influence has grown. Yet the need for meaningful dialogue and information about this diverse region has never been greater. Over the past seven decades, Tuttle has published thousands of books on subjects ranging from martial arts and paper crafts to language learning and literature—and our talented authors, illustrators, designers and photographers have won many prestigious award. We welcome you to explore the wealth of information available on Asia at **www.tuttlepublishing.com.**

Published by Tuttle Publishing, an imprint of Periplus Editions (HK) Ltd.

www.tuttlepublishing.com

JIBUN TO IU KABE JIBUN NO KOKORO NI FURIMAWASARENAI 29 NO HOHO

English translation by Makiko Itoh.

ISBN 978-4-8053-1943-7

28 27 26 25 5 4 3 2 1 2506CM
Printed in China

Distributed by:

North America, Latin America & Europe
Tuttle Publishing
364 Innovation Drive
North Clarendon
VT 05759 9436, USA
Tel: 1(802) 773 8930
Fax: 1(802) 773 6993
info@tuttlepublishing.com
www.tuttlepublishing.com

Asia Pacific
Berkeley Books Pte Ltd
3 Kallang Sector #04-01,
Singapore 349278
Tel: (65) 6741-2178
Fax: (65) 6741-2179
inquiries@periplus.com.sg
www.tuttlepublishing.com

Japan
Tuttle Publishing
Yaekari Building, 3rd Floor
5-4-12 Osaki, Shinagawa-ku
Tokyo 141 0032 Japan
Tel: 81 (3) 5437 0171
Fax: 81 (3) 5437 0755
sales@tuttle.co.jp
www.tuttle.co.jp